Also by Marjorie Harris

Favorite Gardening Tips
Favorite Perennials
Favorite Annuals
Favorite Flowering Shrubs
Favorite Shade Plants
In the Garden: Thoughts on Changing Seasons
The Healing Garden

Pocket Gardening

Pocket Gardening
A Guide to Gardening in Impossible Places

Marjorie Harris

Photographs by Tim Saunders

HarperCollins*PublishersLtd*

POCKET GARDENING: A GUIDE TO GARDENING IN IMPOSSIBLE PLACES. Copyright © 1998 by Marjorie Harris. All rights reserved. No part of this book may be used or reproduced in any manner whatsoever without prior written permission except in the case of brief quotations embodied in reviews. For information address HarperCollins Publishers Ltd, Suite 2900, Hazelton Lanes, 55 Avenue Road, Toronto, Canada M5R 3L2.

http://www.harpercollins.com/canada

First edition

Canadian Cataloguing in Publication Data

Harris, Marjorie
    Pocket gardening : a guide to gardening in impossible places

Includes bibliographical references and index.

ISBN 0-00-638510-9

1. Gardening.   I. Title

SB454.H37 1998   635.9′67   C97-932331-2

98 99 00 ❖ WEB 10 9 8 7 6 5 4 3 2

Printed and bound in Canada

Printed on 20% recycled, acid-free paper

For Sheree-Lee and Chris

Contents

Acknowledgments

Thanks to all the gardeners who allowed themselves to be interviewed and let us into their gardens, which are such a treat. They are Gloria Bishop (whose balcony is on the cover), Jan Sugarman, Dennis Winters and his client Hy Rosenberg, Temma Gentles, Victor Levin, Joanne Clarke, Peter Jackman and Mark McLaine, Keith and Carolyn Squires, Amy and Clair Stewart, Elizabeth Knowles, Ted Johnston, Barbara Sears, Larry Davidson (who has one of my favorite nurseries, Lost Horizons) and Toto Soegandi.

Thanks to Tim Saunders for his wonderful companionship and photography. Ted Johnston not only did major research for this book, he was a constant cheerleader through the whole thing. Karen York edited it with her unusual sensitivity to and vast knowledge of gardening. Iris Tupholme at HarperCollins, as always, is the best person to have on your side while writing a book. And Jack, of course, who has to put up with me talking about gardening all the time.

Introduction

Gardening is easy for the obsessed, filled with wonder for the ingenious, and a trial if you don't know how to start. When I see how clever the really determined gardener is, I am filled with admiration. And that's what led me to write this book. To honor, celebrate and find what impels those gardeners who insist on gardening in the most impossible places. Little pockets of soil anywhere, in any climate, are grist for a gardener's mill. Pocket gardens, as I've come to think of this fascinating way of gardening.

Gardens don't exist in nature *per se*. It's giving shape and form to what goes into the soil that makes up a garden. This can be a total contradiction to what goes on in nature. Paddle a canoe into the most remote wilderness and you'll see a cliffside with a miniature birch tree growing right in the rock. But that isn't a garden, it's one plant's struggle for survival.

That struggle isn't going on merely in remote places.

Observe the lowly sidewalk where no one has swept, hosed down or added chemicals to the cracks, and you'll see a plant (oh, all right, call it a weed) pushing its way to sunlight. I've found lady's mantle, columbine and asters among the plants in my own brick walk. I cannot bear to rip them out, because watching them hang in there is one of the great pleasures of being alive.

It also gives me time to pause and think about the amazing tenacity of a seed to float on a puff of wind or to work its way through an animal's system and fall on fertile ground. Survival is everything to a seed. And watching all this is significant to me, too.

I need the process of gardening to keep me going. I know the quality of my own survival depends on my being able to muck about in the soil. So there is a certain symbiosis here. I can't survive without plants, and most plants in a little pocket won't survive for long without a caregiver.

What follows are the pocket gardens I've found over years of going into gardens, snooping around other people's backyards and being astounded by the gardens that people can build anywhere, in any place.

Throughout, I'll be referring to the garden, and by that I mean all the different categories in the book from a converted parking lot, to containers, to balconies, to a raised bed. I consider all of them gardens as well as being important components of any garden.

You can use this book to build a garden, or you can use it to make a pocket garden on your apartment balcony, in a small unpromising place beside the house or along a dusty unused corridor. For tenants, a pocket garden can be an inexpensive way to add some aesthetic to a temporary space.

If you can't find a chapter for your problem, look it up in the index and you'll find a solution somewhere in this book, I hope. I've mentioned plants all through the text, but most plant information is in Chapter 11, where I talk about what plants to grow and how to look after them.

As we become more crammed into cities, jammed closer and closer together, we'll have to rethink just what constitutes a garden. The huge suburban lot, the deep yards of the inner city or the vast tracts of a country property may eventually be things of the past.

I look over the city I live in and see empty rooftops everywhere, and to me, they are future gardens. I look at dinky little balconies, dirty little corners, alleys, parking lots and see them bulging with potential.

So much of gardening is about attitude, and if your attitude is one of determination to make something beautiful, to leave a place better than you found it, pocket gardening is for you.

One of the funniest pocket gardens I've ever seen isn't far from my own house. The owner planted a huge weeping tree in the postage-stamp-sized patch in front of the house. The tree, as could be expected, grew to the height of the house and spread up and over the street. It is now trimmed very carefully at the bottom so as not to hit the roof, the top of the porch, the person walking from the house, the person walking along the street and the truck driving by on the road—all at different levels. Labor-intensive and highly risible. Every so often, I like to look at it and remind myself that the old gardening saw of right plant, right place is a very important principle.

I have this simple childlike faith that if everyone gardened, we would change dramatically in our attitude to life as well as to nature itself—innocence renewed. I don't think we would be so careless about the planet. We would love and treasure it, rather than feel we have the right to plunder it. We'd demand changes to the cavalier notion that sees Nature as an empty space only Man can fill.

In North America, as Joni Mitchell pointed out decades ago, we took paradise and turned it into a parking lot. I see this all around me in the city. Small front yards given to the car. Nifty backyards covered in tarmac for cars. Inconvenient trees chopped down, messy shrubs razed for parking. We've so successfully hacked away at our forests the whole climate of North America has been modified. As a result, we choke on our excesses.

Gardening in difficult places makes you appreciate the struggle for survival that nature has gone through in these millennia. Garden anywhere, everywhere. Just be sure to garden somewhere. It will change your life, improve your attitude and make you a better person all around.

1

Designing the Pocket Garden

The theory behind this book is that you can garden anywhere. No matter what space is available, the minute you put a plant into soil, you redefine gardening. This fact has become my definition of a garden: one plant and one place just as long as a hand, a brain, an imagination is involved. A pocket garden reflects just that: a small space that demands a plant—a plant that can be put there by an experienced gardener or a tyro.

A pocket garden can be a small area that is quite special in the context of a larger garden, or it can comprise all the space that you've been allotted in this world. It could also be a really tough spot that demands innovative solutions; or any place with a special need of its own.

This may be a tricky way to garden. For one thing, a shallow place, rock-bound soil, a pot or a container will need customized watering. A plant by its very nature makes demands. It needs light, and it's necessary to know exactly how much (two, three, five, ten hours a day?) and what kind (direct, filtered, morning, afternoon?). It's wise to gather this information before you start out.

Designing a pocket garden requires just as much thought and planning as any other garden. Throwing plants willy-nilly into a small space won't make it look gorgeous. Building from a good infrastructure (anything hard, such as paths, fences, patios, walls and trelliswork) will make all else seem easy; creative planting will be an added fillip.

You can also be a renegade in a pocket garden. The rules of garden design are meant to be broken when working in cramped quarters. The most enchanting aspect of pocket gardening is that you can have a jumble of plants tumbling about each other—something which might be revolting on a large scale may look fabulous in a small space. You can train your eye on what goes well together, but you will probably end up with a mix of all your favorite colors—another luxury. Keep in mind that it's possible to build an exciting repertoire of plants within even the most limited boundaries.

The first principle is to divide up the space into as many smaller spaces within the garden as possible. This will make a pocket garden appear larger. Make sure there are open areas (these could be a deck or patio), and clear out anything that's irrelevant, such as old, unattractive trees and shrubs. Begin with as clean a slate as you can. Then start designing.

SCALE

Gardening in a small space means that any mistake is inevitably going to be a glaring one. It's better to plan ahead than to retrofit the design. I've learned this from long and hard experience. When I go crashing about outside, whether it's making a new border or figuring out what to do with containers, I tend to make haste when I should be sitting and quietly thinking things through. The older I get, of course, the more this wisdom sinks in and the more I'm inclined to use less energy and more brain in my gardening.

In all garden design, scale is everything. In pocket gardens, scale becomes even more important, perhaps because it's possible to absorb the whole at once. And it's that first glance which draws the viewer in to look at the garden more intimately.

You'll know immediately when something is out of scale: It seems awkward or just doesn't look right. You examine it from every angle and finally figure it out: too big, too small, too angled, too rounded, all wrong for the site. This is okay if you are working with something tiny, such as a rock or a shell, but when it comes to larger items, it's crucial to get it right first time out. The big stuff, the important stuff, may be anything from a valuable piece of sculpture to a treasured old find from a barn. Out of whack, it will not only look uncomfortable, it will make you feel that way, too.

Scale certainly applies to furnishings. You aren't going to be able to indulge in that fabulous Lutyens three-seater bench, but perhaps a chair in the same style might fit in. A self-circulating stream may be crazy, but a little pond with a bubbling fountain would be just right. Paring down your ambition and longing is a matter of great significance in a pocket garden. Keep in mind that less really is more in a small site.

PRIVACY

My problem has always been one of privacy and that's something to deal with immediately. Alas, for many years, I had a nasty neighbor who wouldn't let me plant vines on one fence ("They are rotting the fence," he said, as he pulled out clematis and honeysuckle). When you look at my garden, it seems to be denser on one side than the other because it is. I missed having that covering, but now I have perfect neighbors, and the fence has filled up, spilling over on their side—to our mutual pleasure.

✦ Check with your neighbors to see just how much latitude you have in your plan for the garden. If they hate the fence design you have your heart set on, you're in trouble and will have to go for a compromise. In most places, it's a given that the cost of fences on mutual boundaries must be shared by neighbors. My solution on the south side was to pay for all of the fence, but I didn't have complete control of the design. On the north side of the house, things worked out much better because it was worked out together aesthetically. At one point in my small garden (though larger than pocket size), we had five different fence styles. These have slowly been eliminated, but had there been some kind of agreement all those decades ago, we would have had a much handsomer environment for the plants.

No one talks about neighbors and gardening, probably because it's such a painful subject. When you have good ones, life can be bliss. Mean neighbors can make gardening a hell, so work it out carefully; don't just go ahead assuming you can do whatever you want to your own property.

Walls and Fences

Think of the garden as a room, and it becomes obvious that the first thing you should deal with is the walls. If you have stone walls, you are fortunate. They provide warmth for plants; you can even plant right in the stonework, and create a microclimate for plants at the base at the same time. If you are having stone walls or terracing installed, make sure there are pockets of soil to tuck plants into.

The most desirable "room divider" or backdrop, especially in the city, is a high hedge to provide sound absorption and maximum privacy. Failing that, a fence or wall covered with vines is the next best thing. In a small garden, the fence design is critical because it can be—quite literally—in your face.

✦ Don't go for cheap in this regard. Use only good material on fences. They should last for decades. Cedar is a superb, long-lasting wood and, with proper preparation, weathers to a fine gray patina. If you use a stain, experiment with different shades and never accept the merely trendy. I left one painter to his own devices and lived for a time with a strange, exotic green never seen in nature. To tone down this abomination, I had a carpenter build 14-inch-square lattice over the fence and immediately smothered it in fast-growing annual vines along with slower-growing perennials (see page 86 for my choices).

✦ If you can't get a fence high enough to give you a true sense of privacy, extend it beyond the strictly legal limit by adding trelliswork to the top (again, mutually agreed upon with neighbors).

✦ The style of the fence should meld or harmonize with the style of the house. A picket fence doesn't go with a Japanese-style garden. By the same token, garden structures should also fit in naturally with the architecture of the house and garden: using the same material, for example (clapboard house = clapboard shed or storage space). The shape of the house should also have an influence on the shape of these tiny outbuildings. Make a gate similar to a door, or have a trellis screen echo the trellis on the fence. Paint them the same color as the house or its trim. Using the same materials, even the same stain, can add just the right touch of visual harmony needed in cramped spaces.

✦ There are many styles that work well in a pocket garden; any kind of trelliswork open enough to let light through and yet support plants for privacy is probably the easiest solution. But don't overlook the many other styles of fencing, from grape stakes to old logs.

✦ Horizontal wooden screening will keep a small garden from feeling claustrophobic. The more open you make your fencing, the more you'll be borrowing the view of your neighbors' gardens. This may be a good thing; on the other hand, you could be looking into a collection of rusting old cars. Take either into consideration when you choose a fence style.

✦ Plant vines as soon as the fence is completed—even before you tackle the rest of the garden. This will give a more settled look to raw space.

Paths

Paths can be just about the most difficult part of the garden to decide upon. In my experience, you put them in once—it's just too expensive to change things after they've been completed.

✦ Flagstone is very attractive and very expensive, and unless you have the experience, get an expert to install it. Flagstones must be laid on a level base of sand, and you should add sandy soil between the cracks to fill in with plants (absolutely necessary in my opinion).

✦ Use flagstones as edgers to beds or gravel paths.

✦ Gravel is a wonderful path material, but then, in a small space, perhaps river rock, which is much more expensive, isn't an extravagance.

✦ Wooden slats on slight risers can make a good transition from one part of the garden to another.

✦ A very small garden may need only large stones as stepping pads. They look really natural once surrounded by plants.

The View

If you've got a perfectly divine view (the Mediterranean Sea would be nice) or someone else's incredible tree, you can build on either as a focal point. If, however, a hideous garage looms large, start to plan immediately how you'll disguise it. One attractive resolution to this problem is to give the garage a face lift to reflect the design of the house. Another is to transform it into a small cottage with a simple paint job, decent trim about the door and windows, and let roses crawl all over the surface.

Neighboring garages are another matter. You can screen them out with vines, large shrubs or carefully placed small trees. Adding a wall of trellis can also look handsome. On one side of my own garden, I can see a dreadful garage—too big, too white—and no chance of changing things. Part of my life is figuring out how to blot out this desecration. A cedar has been planted to help hide it, but it will take at least a decade to be effective. At the moment, nothing seems sufficient. It's this kind of problem to address as you are designing your garden. Don't let it bug you for years. The following applies to any size garden, not just little ones: Get as much collaboration and cooperation with your neighbors as you can when building fences, garages, toolsheds and other outbuildings, such as a swimming pool cabana. These structures are expensive and, once installed, will probably have to fall down before they are changed.

I have seen a splendid solution to neighboring pocket gardens: A toolshed in one has been designed so it makes a pleasing backdrop for a tiny patio on the other. The fence is coordinated with the shed so it looks all of a piece without any element dominating. Views from both houses are elegant and yet each maintains its sense of being self-contained.

On the other hand, you might want to extend your view by tearing down fences and creating a communal garden with your neighbors (Beyond the Pocket Garden). This is always tricky, because one thing you need in a city is privacy. But other things may be more significant to you—a vista, for instance.

It's important to frame the small garden. You can translate this almost any way you want: how you see it from windows facing the garden; what kind of fencing you choose; what artifacts or stones and/or special specimen plants will be central to the design. Most gardeners want instant results; achieve this with the hard stuff, such as patio, walls, treillage. This endows the space with strength and will make plant choices that much easier. And it's those plant choices that will ultimately make the garden what it is.

ILLUSIONS

One of the smartest moves I made to create an illusion of width in my garden was adding mirrors. While it does mean that the one on the deck startles first-time visitors and tempts people to fuss with hair or makeup, the mirror makes the area feel twice as wide as it actually is. What it reflects is a piece of sculpture on the opposite wall and much greenery.

Mirrors can be used on their own and framed by plants or placed behind a grate or trelliswork. This adds density to the elements in the garden without making them appear fussy. A mirror along one fence is echoed across the way on the opposite fence for a riveting effect. Or, if you have a strategically placed window, a mirror placed on an angle so that it reflects the garden back into the house would be dramatic.

One principle that doesn't change with the size of a garden is to keep part of it secret. Don't reveal everything at once. You can merely hint that there may be something beyond. A *faux* gate built into a fence, for instance, gives the feeling that this is an antechamber to the garden and creates a slightly grander appearance without being pretentious.

I put a large shrub—a species rose, *Rosa glauca*— close to the deck at the back of our house. It acts as a scrim or curtain that you have to look through and move around to get to the rest of the garden, though in essence, this is not a large space.

Here are a number of other tricks that you can use to give the illusion of space:

+ False perspective: A pond with the end closest to the house larger than the far end will make the pond seem to extend much farther.

+ Put large pots at the front of a small garden; smaller pots and plants behind them will appear to be farther away.

+ Make a path appear longer by placing smaller and smaller plants along the edges as they recede into the distance.

+ Change levels. This is easily the most satisfying way to create a sense of space. One of the prettiest little gardens I've seen was on a slight slope. The owners had the garden dug down, replaced the heavy clay with good soil and built wide steps going into the main space. It has a rather grand feeling to it, even though it's only a matter of a few feet.

✦ Build up the sides of borders to create raised beds, and put in tall plants for a dramatic change of pace.

✦ Use an arch or bower to get from one part of the garden to another, effectively making a secret garden. It may only be a small place with a garden chair, but it will *feel* as though it's larger. Have the arch dripping with vines so that you get the benefit of a succession of bloom. This will be not only a focal point but also a barrier that you have to pass through to go beyond, creating an amorphous and therefore more mysterious effect.

✦ If you have a dark corner, paint it white or some very pale stain. The light bounces back and makes a wall or fence appear to fall away.

✦ To make a space appear much larger, add an object such as a sculpture or an obelisk that is quite big, then smother it with greenery. It will appear to be growing out of the vegetation and seem to be farther away.

✦ Or do the converse: Put something quite small on a plinth or other riser, and keep the greenery on a very low scale. The object will appear to erupt from the soil and move away from the viewer's eye.

✦ See Jan Sugarman's alley (shot #1) for a graceful entrance to a small garden. Here, the gardener proves that no space has to be unwelcoming if you add plants. In a boring, narrow alley between two houses, Jan Sugarman put one pot, which was joined by another, then another, and soon, she had a small alley garden. She chose plants that would give off scent, such as eucalyptus (which she brings indoors in the winter). As she has proved, you can grow almost anything anywhere with the proper attention.

✦ Add height to the garden not only to lend a sense of privacy but also to make you feel that it soars. Tall, slender trees such as poplar and birch will certainly provide a feeling of airiness. You can achieve a more modest effect by adding trelliswork to the top of a fence to increase privacy and enhance the sense of enclosure important to a small garden.

✦ In even the smallest pocket garden, make sure there's a place for seating, if only for one person. It will contribute a sense of purpose and an element of serenity. Make it secluded and give cooling shade by surrounding the area with large plants.

✦ To create an illusion of space, put things on angles so that they don't all appear at once. This could apply to the way patio stones are set or to a path designed to make raised beds. Not everything has to be on strict rectilinear forms. One designer I have in mind used all his infrastructure—in this case, the trellis, the paving, the edges of raised beds constructed in a diamond shape—to give much more depth to the garden. Then the whole was filled with miniature versions of well-known plants—*Rosa* 'The Fairy' with a dwarf cotoneaster, for example.

✦ Don't be afraid to jam in as many plants as possible.

Not only will it be a surprise to the outsider, it will also give your eye that much more to rest on. Make subtle waves of color rather than drifts of any specific plant. The concept of having three, five or seven of any one plant just has to be ignored in most tiny gardens.

✦ Lighting: tricky and absolutely necessary. Where there are long winters, a well-placed light or two will give any garden drama. I have a low-growing Japanese maple lit from beneath with a small, upfacing black lamp. It looks magnificent under a blanket of snow. We really need nothing else, though at the back of the garden, a birch with its fine, white bark is also lit up at night. Be careful when illuminating trees. You might place the lights so that everyone in the neighborhood will be irritated. Watch how the halo swings out and where it's traveling to.

STORAGE SPACE

Finding place for storage in tiny spaces is the act of a wizard—or good garden design. One of the most graceful solutions I've seen is a storage space and fence united as a single unit. Using the fence as backing, the narrow, sloping roof, shallow side walls and sliding doors below the top of the fence create a place for equipment, bikes and toys. It is so well integrated into the facade of the fence that you barely notice it.

We have an alley between our house and the house

next door. Near the back of the house is a slightly wider space where we had a little shed built. It's raised off the ground by about 3 inches, with a solid floor. This means I've got a safe, protected spot to keep valued containers all winter long. It's just large enough to store all the garden equipment, but so snug that storing any new purchases means something has to be discarded or given away. Cuts down on my spending as well.

GRASS

I have a reputation for being crabby about grass. I don't really hate grass; I hate what we pour all over it to have perfect grass. Thankfully, in a pocket garden, there will be barely enough room for grass. If you insist on a tiny little patch, just for a visual element, that's fine, but think about how you will cut it. Certainly not with a big machine. Clippers? Do you really want to expend that much energy when you could have a dozen more plants? There's no argument as far as I'm concerned. So you might as well get rid of it.

+ What grass you have to pull up can be easily composted by turning it over and blanketing it with a layer of manure. You'll be able to plant on this mini-berm or rise pretty quickly, and once it's clad with other plants and groundcovers, you'll never know it was once ratty-looking grass.
+ If you do decide to keep a small patch of grass, give it a good feed of compost in spring and fall. This

will keep it healthy and you won't have to douse it with chemicals.

PROBLEM SPACES

Most pocket gardens have to deal with such problems as limited light, terrible soil, cramped spaces. In the next chapter, I deal with soil, but light is a factor that must be considered when you first start to design your garden. To help solve the problems, prepare the soil properly and then proceed as follows:

Dark Passageways

✦ Any passage can be improved with a little pocket-gardening moxie. A dark entranceway to the basement or a side entrance you want people to use can be improved with some decent paint in a lively and compelling color. Here's where gardening as illusion can take place. One of the best new, though very old, methods of raising a dark place into the sun is *trompe l'oeil.* This painting technique makes any surface look like something else (it fools the eye). In Nice, France, this is such an important tradition that whole courtyards are created in paint, complete with windows and shutters that you'd swear were real. Vistas painted onto walls are found almost everywhere. I've seen the most enchanting use of this in a garden house. The

1

Jan Sugarman's alley garden has a combination of scented eucalyptus and annuals. See pages 12 and 111 for a complete description.

2

Artist Joanne Clarke composes her containers the way she does a canvas. She tries out all the new forms of coleus each year, and has a base of golden hops and *Helichrysum petiolare* (the gray foliage). Scented geraniums and masses of heliotrope and scaevola add to this lucious mix. The climbing hydrangea going up the face of the house makes a sensual background. See page 43.

back of the little structure was painted with a vision of fields in the distance and the owners' two dogs lounging in the foreground. It opened up a whole shady little area. Painting an opening into a fence can also add a bit of mystery.

✦ A dark, narrow passage at the side of the house can be transformed into a charming space by adding the focal point of an urn on a plinth; then put in a gravel walk edged by shade-loving plants.

✦ I'm always astonished at the number of plants you can get into a very small space. You can be as diverse as your imagination makes possible in a way that on a larger scale would look dreadful. For instance, stuffing a couple of dozen plants into a dark area such as a side passageway can bring enormous life to it. Get your mind around the idea that this is a courtyard and something to be dealt with on its own (though relating to any other garden it connects with). First, you must get to know your shade-loving plants (see Chapter 11). Then put them together with a graceful design and foliage color pattern in mind. For instance, I happen to love the combination of blue and yellow, and plants with these colors of foliage perk up a dark spot wonderfully.

✦ Evergreen ferns such as Christmas fern, *Polystichum acrostichoides*; ebony spleenwort, *Asplenium platyneuron*; and maidenhair spleenwort, *A. trichomanes*, make a good background for the intense blues of hostas such as *H.* 'Blue Cadet,'

'Halcyon' or 'Blue Lake.' Put in a few bright yellow edger hostas such as 'Limelight,' 'Gold Edger,' 'Feather Boa' and 'Golden Sceptre.' Add an eye-popping variegated brunnera, and you've got a great start. A blue corydalis such as *C. flexuosa* 'Blue Panda' will bring any visitor to a dead halt.

✦ One of the best ways of having a permanent but almost invisible support for vines is to use heavy-gauge fishing line. It's indestructible, and you can loop it through eyehooks up a wall, overhead to form a ceiling or along a metal stairway.

✦ For permanent plantings such as perennial vines, construct a box or container larger than 18 inches in all directions so that the root system will be protected during winter freeze-thaws.

Long, Narrow Spaces

✦ Little gardens are often long and narrow. One superb method of space-saving disguise is the 18th-century art of espalier. This is training a plant flat against the wall of a house or on a fence in a pattern that will mask what's behind it and still leave space in front for yet another group of plants to be used efficiently. It's relatively easy, and you will find it quite a lot of fun to maintain.

See page 173 for how to do it and what to do it to. Espaliered plants such as roses, dwarf fruit trees and firethorn, *Pyracantha*, create a good background for all the other plants, add height and give the illusion that there is more, much more beyond.

✦ Emphasize the long, narrow aspect by making a checkerboard pattern with patio stones. I did this, and immediately, the garden had strength, a way to move through it that was unconventional and plenty of tiny pockets, each of which has its own flavor. The whole becomes a tapestry that gives major impact.

THE PLANTING

✦ You have to keep several things in mind. First, absolutely no monoplanting (all one color, all one texture) in a pocket garden. You must have something going on all year round, or this small space will drive you crazy. Nothing but daylilies would be utterly boring for quite a large part of the year. Ditto with nothing but evergreens. It's a joyous mix of evergreen and deciduous trees and shrubs, woody and herbaceous perennials, some annuals for instant color, plus a complete underplanting of bulbs that you want.

✦ Trees and shrubs will provide the skeleton of your design, and give it even more shape. Large, columnar trees such as cedars may blot out something you'd rather not see, but remember, they scoop huge amounts of nutrition all around the trunks and will require raised beds to make as much room as possible for other plants.

THE SEASONS

SPRING

Designing for spring automatically means bulbs. My ideal is a carpet of bulbs in harmonizing colors that all come out at the same time and last for at least a month. It's an ideal and nothing else. Start by having the spaces where you might be walking filled with early-spring snowdrops, *Galanthus*, which really do come out when snow is on the ground; winter aconites, *Eranthis*, like drops of sunlight; scilla and grape hyacinths, *Muscari*, in cobalt blue. This is a basic blue-and-yellow combination, and they'll have a few moments of overlapping. Adding the larger bulbs such as tulips and narcissus in a really tiny area is, to my mind, a waste of space. Put these big bulbs into containers, where you can easily see them. Then move them out of the way when they inevitably pass into their yellowing phase (see Chapter 3 on container gardening).

Spring-flowering shrubs are a must: Serviceberry, *Amelanchier*, has delicate white blossoms that turn into berries which are edible by both people and birds. Other good spring blooms can be had from lilacs, *Syringa*, including dwarf forms ideal for a pocket garden; cherry, *Prunus*; crab apple, *Malus* 'Red Jade'; and the star magnolia, *Magnolia stellata*, an utterly charming spring shrub that won't get too large.

SUMMER

This is the time for perennials to really shine. My list of smallish perennials is endless, but don't overlook planting annuals for some solid color as well. This can be done in containers so that you can move them around and fill in holes left by dying bulbs.

Expand your space with summer-flowering bulbs such as dahlias, caladiums and dwarf lilies in pots, a miniature herb garden or even a small salad garden in a medium-sized tub.

Summer-flowering shrubs have their place as well. Summersweet, *Clethra alnifolia*, comes in both white and pink forms. *Kirengeshoma palmata* and *K. koreana* are both subtle, with very small but totally exquisite yellow trumpets hanging from the end of elegant stems with attractive maplelike leaves; and the most glorious of all, the oak-leaf hydrangea, *Hydrangea quercifolia*—what a plant, with great blooms in summer and breathtaking fall color.

AUTUMN

The first absolute necessity in the autumn garden is the use of ornamental grasses. They will provide not only color (from a deep steely blue to bright red to the richness of burnt sienna) but also sound. The cruel winds of autumn seem less fierce when they are moving the graceful plumes of a grass. And most of these splendid plants will last throughout the winter. With all grasses, you need to leave space, and you need to whack them right back in spring. Other than that, there is little they require except occasional watering.

WINTER

I don't normally overtidy my own garden, so there is a lot of winter interest in it. This has a number of benefits: It provides forage for birds; the stems and seedheads make patterns in the snow; and the stalks protect the plants below.

Ornamental grasses will look good through spring. I particularly favor blue oat grass, *Helictotrichon sempervirens*, which is a brilliant blue and stands erect all winter long. Here are some others that have a good winter presence and won't become grossly large: little bluestem, *Andropogon scoparius*, snowy wood rush, *Luzula nivea*, and tufted hair grass, *Deschampsia caespitosa*.

Any pocket garden can benefit from having at least two to three small evergreen shrubs to give the winter garden some real guts. Add evergreens right after you've installed vines. Think about the colors, shapes and textures you'll be having at very close proximity. You can find evergreens in almost every shape and size; just make sure you don't get something gross, like a blue spruce that will reach 100 feet in height and 25 feet in width. If your winters are really long, plant evergreens in a pattern. Up to one-third of the space given over to some of the dwarf and colored species will make a pleasant vista during the bare times.

Even a small space can be turned into a woodland with ferns, hostas, trees and shrubs. I like using some of the broad-leaved evergreens such as mountain laurel, *Kalmia latifolia,* lily-of-the-valley bush, *Pieris japonica,* and very hardy rhododendrons. Groundcovers such as European ginger and ivy will tolerate shade and look shiny and new right up until spring. See Chapter 11 for more suggestions.

Any small tree with interesting bark such as the soft gray of ginkgo, coralbark maple, *Acer palmatum* 'Sango Kaku' or 'Senkaki,' or paperbark maple, *A. griseum,* will make a lovely winter statement.

As for shrubs, Oregon grape, *Mahonia aquifolium,* is, hands down, one of the best winter plants for a cold climate. Its one drawback is that, in early spring, it looks dreadful for several weeks. Resist the temptation to either prune it or yank it out. It will return.

Deep black-green, dense and almost unkillable, yews are the garden's best backdrop plant. I like to put red-stalked plants such as Siberian dogwood or coralbark maple in front.

Look for dwarf forms of evergreen plants such as yew, *Taxus;* dwarf balsam fir, *Abies balsamea* 'Nana'; dwarf white fir, *A. concolor* 'Compacta'; bog rosemary, *Andromeda polifolia;* rose daphne, *Daphne cneorum;* and inkberry, *Ilex glabra.* None will overwhelm a small garden, and the shapes are wonderful.

2

Prepping the Pocket Garden

Over the years I've gardened, the most profound lesson I've learned is that good preparation is an absolute must. Successful gardening depends on it. You can even buy plants that aren't in the best of condition (abused plants, indeed), and, with superb prep, you can bring them into a healthy state and grow them well.

In fact, the more gardens I visit each year, the more I admire good growing. You can see it shine out of plants, much the way a healthy skin glows. Good growing comes from deep composting and meticulous mulching. No matter how much space is available for growing, there should be a space for a compost pile.

Among other essentials, the main one is knowing your site. Listening and learning from it will pay off in the end. Why impose an English cottage garden on a piece of the Canadian Shield or a Saskatchewan prairie when it's so clearly growing against the grain? Give your plants the very best chance for survival by looking to what you actually have and capitalizing on it.

FIRST PRINCIPLES

Pay attention to two details here: light and drainage. They are both next to godliness and are significant elements in successful pocket gardening. You can lump along and slowly improve bad soil, but if your drainage is nonexistent, you won't have much luck with anything.

The first thing, of course, is a major cleanup. Sweep out any muck, and get rid of shrubs or plants that don't come up to what will be your lofty standards. Be ruthless. Just because a plant is old doesn't mean it should hang on forever. On the other hand, a mature plant can give a settled look to any garden. Examine these ancients carefully to see whether they can be pruned into a brilliant new shape. If not, to the trash heap.

Cleanup doesn't mean just a tidy look. Crawl around and make sure chewing enemies aren't lurking out there. Then handpick and squish. Gardening is brutal.

When working with fairly deep shade, make sure there isn't a massive crop of slugs. If so, get out there every day, pick them off and stomp on them.

Light Conditions

The first move is a bit of a challenge. You must count the number of hours of sunlight, where it falls and what quality it is. More difficult than it sounds.

✦ Make a sun map, if you have patience enough and time. Draw up a plan of your garden, and figure out where the sun is at different times of the day (morning, noon, late afternoon, sunset) and at different times of the year. It won't surprise you to find that the low sun in winter hits only very specific parts of the garden, and you should plant for this.

✦ Work out the quality of shade. Don't kid yourself about these categories. They all mean something, and many plants won't grow anywhere else. I've always been disappointed in my own inability to steer clear of sun-loving plants when it's obvious that I have quite a shady garden. But I do find little pockets that get about six hours of sun a day, and I make do. Some plants live to thrive, though it may take a couple of years to adjust to the lower light conditions. Of course, they never reach their full potential. Always remember that shade is complex.

Deep shade. The shade under heavily canopied trees such as mature maples, oaks and (the worst) weeping willows. Dense shade will also be behind a wall, buildings, fences and solid evergreen hedges.

Light or dappled shade. Usually cast by high tree canopies that allow sun to filter through in a soft form at least during the midday. It could also mean an area that gets early-morning or late-afternoon sun. Shade-loving plants prefer this dappled light over all others.

Semi-shade. Areas where the sun hits for only four hours or less a day. Consider carefully when the plants will be in the sun. Late-afternoon sun is much hotter than early-morning sun. You'll want plants that have some sun tolerance and can still handle shade.

✦ Golden, blue and variegated plants or those with huge lush leaves usually like to keep in the shade. Sun can wipe out the very qualities that make them good plants. Pale colors, especially whites, blues and yellows, shine in the shade.

Full sun. Applies to an area getting more than six hours of sun a day. Again, check whether it gets more of the softer morning sun or the intense late-afternoon sun, which can be cruel for plants.

Drainage

This is another of the basics of gardening too often ignored. Many plants will tolerate being out of their range of hardiness if they have superb drainage. You can test this by digging a fairly large hole, pouring in a bucket of water and seeing how long it takes to drain out. If it takes more than half an hour, you have slow drainage and should be adding sand or humus to lighten things up. If it takes hours to drain, you have a problem. There are a number of solutions. You can add masses of composted leaves and sand, or you may have to dig down as far as you can and add layers of sand and gravel. The most efficient thing to do is all of the above, plus make raised beds. Then rebuild them with as much organic matter as possible.

◆ Berming can also help, especially with hard clay or compacted soil with lousy drainage. Dig down as far as you can go and add sand and gravel, then build up layers of leaves, compost and ordinary soil. It will end up making a good-sized mound. Water and let settle before planting. The berm will naturally compost down over the years.

◆ Here's an extreme but absolutely workable solution given to me by a wonderful gardener, Marion Jarvie. She piles up scads of leaves and chopped-up garden wastes, then dampens the whole thing down. On top goes as much fine-grade builder's sand as possible. It may look like the Sahara at first, but as the sand percolates through the organic material, it lightens up the soil. She recommends doing this in the fall. By spring, she guarantees that it will have broken down and you'll have light, friable soil. I've tried it in small areas and it works very, very well. It just takes courage to cover a large area.

✦ Whenever I have the slightest problem with my soil (which tends to be a bit on the heavy, rich side), I now add a layer of sand. It looks odd at first, but eventually, it vanishes.

✦ Sandy soil that drains far too quickly will leave plants gasping for water. Add lots of humus and compost to bump up texture in the soil.

Soil

Soil is the soul of gardening. I may be casual about my gardening habits in some ways, but I'm never casual about soil. I think about it all the time. I can get really absorbed by the complexity of this material which covers the planet and takes so long to develop. It's been estimated that an inch of soil takes about 10,000 years to develop from the pure rock whence it came. I've tried just about every method there is to get the great soil I have today, and the best one of all is piling up humus and letting the worms do the work.

Let me explain. I have rich clay soil, which is full of nutrients but also heavy and, at times, waterlogged. I started one fall by taking a horrible piece of ground and piling up leaves from the garden, plus everything else that seemed worthwhile from our garden and many others (weeds, cut-down plants, grass clippings). This was left to its own resources over the winter. In spring, we added compost. Piling it up as much as possible—about 3 feet—means that anything underneath, including sod, will help rot things down. Then, to accelerate the composting, I added a layer of manure. In cold climates, for quick results, you might want to cover the whole thing with black plastic. Where it isn't terribly cold all winter, you won't have to worry. It may take a bit longer this way, but you can save yourself the backbreaking labor of digging up a new bed.

✦ Intensive planting requires soil rich in humus. So add compost, manure (mushroom, sheep) and leaf mold to give it density.

✦ The alternative is double-digging. I've seen this done exactly once in my gardening life, and then by a gardener trained at Kew Gardens in England. Dig a trench, put the soil to one side. Break up all the hardpan at the bottom. Add plenty of humus (well-rotted leaves are ideal) to the soil, and put it back into the trench. Take the soil out of one trench, and use it to fill in the previous one, working your way down the bed, filling the last trench with the soil from the first. Keep trenching the area until you end up with a slightly raised bed of friable, easy-to-plant soil. This is an unbelievable amount of work.

✦ I never cultivate, but I do add a lot of stuff to the surface of the soil and let nature and the worms take their course. I hate the idea of messing about around root systems and am appalled at what kind of damage can be perpetrated doing this. I no longer understand why people bother.

COMPOSTING

Compost supplies the much-needed organic material that will condition the soil and act as a fertilizer as it feeds the soil. Extensive trials have now proved that compost is incredibly effective in preventing disease. Gardeners on even the tiniest balcony or roof garden can compost.

You can understand the way compost works merely by observing what happens in the forest. Leaves fall to the ground; they are attacked by microorganisms that break them down into humus, supplying the rich top layer needed to support the trees.

Experiment by making a pile of leaves and other garden detritus, then try to find it in a few months. It will have almost completely disappeared.

General Composting Principles

Just a few things really need to be known about composting. It's a bit like owning a computer—you don't want to know too much, or it will just be confusing. But some information is absolutely essential.

First is decomposition, the process in which all those little microorganisms that you can't see, such as bacteria, molds and fungi, feed on and break down organic material. What these minute animals do is stabilize the soil aggregates as they are slurping up all this material. They need just the right amount of moisture (not dripping wet) and mass. When there's lots of activity, they create humus that improves the soil structure. This makes for better drainage, increases the amount of oxygen getting to root systems and distributes nutrients.

All this happens in a stately and very orderly process. But you should know a little about the carbon-to-nitrogen ratio. Carbon comes from leaves, straw, hay (brown); nitrogen is generated by grass clippings, coffee grounds, garden detritus, manure (green). To have the most efficient pile possible, create layers in the compost. Think green and brown. Green = nitrogen. Brown = carbon.

In the first stage, the microorganisms feed on carbon, nitrogen and proteins. The more there is of the first, the faster this will happen. The pile heats up. Then in the second stage, the microorganisms consume the organic material, the carbon-to-nitrogen ratio falls, the activity of breaking down slows, and humus is produced. The pile cools down.

Other ingredients—phosphorus, potassium and trace minerals—will come from kitchen wastes, such as apple peels, potato skins, eggshells, banana skins and orange rinds.

You'll be able to tell when the compost is almost finished—it starts to look like the best soil you've ever seen. Spread around the garden, it will act as an excellent mulch to protect the surface of the soil.

There's no particular magic in any one composter that I've found, but I tend to like ones that are made of wood, with lots of space between the slats for air to circulate through the heap. A critical mass must be achieved for a compost pile to work effectively, however. Unless you've got space for something that's 3 feet by 3 feet, you should try vermicomposting, which takes up little room and is very effective.

Vermicomposting

If I lived in an apartment, I would practice vermiculture or vermicomposting, a form of indoor composting that relies only on what worms will do to your garbage. Having thousands of worms at work under the kitchen counter scares a lot of people. But don't be thrown off. It comprises a plastic composter with drainage holes for moisture and air holes along the side. The worms live in nests made by you, and there is no possibility that they'll escape (they hate light and love the dark, moist atmosphere the vermicomposter provides), so even the squeamish can do this.

◆ Make initial nests with torn-up newspaper, and slowly add kitchen wastes, chopped up very fine if you want fast action. It will turn into a brown, soil-like substance almost before your eyes. It will also leach out a dense liquid, so make sure you have a container under the composter to catch it. This is very rich compost tea and should be cut in half before being used to water indoor plants during the winter or container plants the rest of the year.

Using Compost

If you don't have ideal friable loam, start mixing compost in with what you've got and then top-dress. That is, add a couple of inches of compost to the top of the soil.

+ Rules of thumb: The warmer the area you live in, the more you're going to need. The wetter your area, the more you'll need.
+ A cubic yard of compost covers 324 square feet to a depth of 1 inch.
+ A cubic yard contains 27 cubic feet.
+ A cubic foot covers 12 square feet to a depth of 1 inch.

Once you've got good soil, add a 1-inch layer of compost every year to maintain the soil health.

MAINTENANCE

+ Stake anything grand: Use bamboo stakes painted green, or lengths of rebar, a half-inch rolled-steel bar that can do many things. Make tepees out of it, or create crossbar holders by forming a triangle with two bars and laying another across the crotches.
+ Twigging up: a fine English term for propping plants without using plastic. Cut up vines such as wild grape, and bend them into half-moons to prop up beans; it's possible to weave them into peony supports. Save twigs and branches from pruning shrubs and trees to hold floppy perennials in place.

SPRING

As soon as the soil warms up, start getting all your need-to-tidy hormones outside. Now is the time to cut back perennials and to rake up the leaves left in place over winter. But be sure to save anything you scrape off the surface of the garden to finish off quickly in the composter.

✦ Prune shrubs and trees that bloom in the autumn or on new wood. Shape the plant, but don't take out more than one-quarter to one-third of the plant's bulk. Do this from the center (never the outside), and move outward. Nip off the dead, the ugly and the crisscrossed branches. Don't touch the spring-flowering plants until *after* they have bloomed, then proceed as above. If you work your way through the garden taking out from one-quarter to one-third of a plant, it will never be obvious how much you've shaved off and you'll have shrubs and trees constantly renewing themselves without getting out of hand and overwhelming a small space.

✦ This is the time to coppice, another good English term. It means cutting a shrub (usually) down almost to the ground. This takes courage, but most plants bound back in the full flush of youth very quickly. Or they die. I tried this on a 30-year-old burning bush, *Euonymus alata*, that had lost its oomph. What a dramatic change. It looks like a brand-new plant. Coppicing is a pretty drastic rejuvenation measure but can be done regularly on such shrubs as golden elders, *Sambucus*, and purple smoketrees, *Cotinus coggygria*, to get the brightest leaf color.

✦ Dividing perennials is fun to do in spring when you are fresh and the plants are relatively small. Some, such as peonies, however, should be left until autumn for this chore. Divide early in the morning, never at midday or during a heat wave. The idea is to keep stress levels for both gardener and plant as low as possible.

Dig up the plant so enough soil is left around the roots to afford some protection. With a sharp spade (for large plants) or trowel, make a quick plunge into the middle of the plant and pull both sides apart. It seems painful, but plants recover quickly if you get them into a well-prepared site as quickly as possible. Otherwise, pop them into a container, and keep it in the shade until you're ready to replant.

✦ Cut back roses by about a third if you think they need it.

✦ Small containers can be emptied into the composter and refilled for a fresh season. Clean them up, soak, and cover the drainage hole before planting. Really large wooden or frost-resistant containers—more than 18 inches—can be left and compost added to the top to refresh the soil. See page 57 for more information.

SUMMER

Most people like to take the summer off from gardening, but not me. I love staying in the city, looking after the garden, and resent invitations for anything that interferes with valuable weekend gardening. This is the time for serious moving around. It's a habit with hazards. I've been astonished when a year off from perpetual motion means the garden does fantastically well without much help from me. It's hard on the ego but a good lesson in stewardship. Sometimes less really is more.

By this time of year, I've got a pretty deep layer of mulch spread around to protect plants from drying out excessively; it certainly makes a nice haven for bugs. But if you think about this as a place to catch them, it cuts the grief in half. Go around the pocket garden handpicking the little blighters.

AUTUMN

I don't scurry about cleaning up all the leaves. I make it look pretty enough without being scrupulous. Leave vines, all plants with seeds, and stalks with hips or berries alone. They are a haven for overwintering birds. This is far more important than putting out bird feeders, which make birds dependent. This way, you give them the food they need without interfering with natural processes. It also means you don't attract the millions of scavenging pigeons—a plague in most cities.

✦ Make sure all evergreens are watered deeply before hard frost—they transpire and lose moisture all winter.

✦ Plant new perennials, especially those that bloom in spring. For any that bloom later than June, plant those one zone hardier than your own.

✦ Plant bulbs everywhere and be sure to tuck them under and around new plants and divisions.

WINTER

This is the ideal time to evaluate what you've got; to analyze carefully the planting patterns that are obvious under the snow. I usually make lists of plants and plant combinations I'd like to try and put them in the daily garden journal I've kept so meticulously for decades. Put these notes in a place where you'll come across them at the right time. Obvious as this may seem, I've spent too much time searching for my deathless concepts not to mention it.

TIPS TO TAKE INTO THE GARDEN

Slug Bait

✦ Here's something nursery people use with great abandon. Mix 1 part of ammonia with 10 parts of water, and pour it over the spaces where slugs may be wintering over. You can do this right over the top of hostas when they first appear in spring—it won't harm the plants.

✦ Leave out saucers full of beer as a trap, and empty regularly.

✦ Combine 1 teaspoon each of honey, vegetable oil and brewer's yeast; mix with enough water to half fill a yogurt container. Again, be sure to empty it regularly.

Cats

✦ If you have problems with cats spraying around certain areas, cut Dettol in half with water and spray the area with the concoction.

Insect Repellent

✦ Combine 1 cup of Skin So Soft (Avon), 1 cup of water and 3 tablespoons apple cider vinegar. Coat your exposed flesh, and no bug will dare get near you.

Harmless Plant Spray

✦ My Auntie Marge says she's used this spray on apple trees and rose bushes and found that the leaves look lovely and glossy and don't get chewed.

Mix the following, and then cut the mixture in half with water:

4 cups water
1 cup rubbing alcohol
$^1/_2$ cup cooking oil
$^1/_2$ tablespoon dishwashing liquid

Use sprays on trees and shrubs only before or after blossoms are out.

3

Containers

A garden without containers is a poor place indeed. The more I garden, the more I use them. Sometimes it's because I want to look into the face of my plants. Or perhaps it's the sheer versatility of pots that make them so enchanting. They can be used to disguise the worst errors in garden design.

Let pots fill in where yellowing bulbs and short-lived perennials leave a hole. Piled up dexterously, they become a sculptural design on a deck or in the garden. They can even create extra space for vegetables in the hard-pressed pocket garden.

Pots can perform just about anywhere in the garden—from the roof to the well of an alley; sitting on a sidewalk; making a stage setting on a deck. If you don't have a garden, they will provide an invaluable service on windowsills, balconies, patios and decks. Look at Joanne Clarke's marvelous arrangement of them on her patios (see shot #2).

You can learn a great deal from working with container plants. For one thing, you can experiment with combinations of plant shapes, foliage textures and types and, most of all, colors. They allow the imagination to take flight in design. Experimentation with color is part of the garden game. Just approaching containers as test grounds can lead you to trying out perennial, rare or exotic plants that you wouldn't try out in the garden itself.

Some principles: Don't think you have to be confined to zonal pelargoniums (the ubiquitous scarlet geranium). You can try anything in a pot just by using some sort of sense. You wouldn't put a silver maple in a container, but there are lots of other trees that you *can* use.

One theory states that you should have only one type of container or pot (say, all terra-cotta) in varying sizes. I don't agree. I like the idea of a collection of pots, each of which has intrinsic value and isn't merely something to hold a whole lot of plants.

Using this method of collection (anything that appeals), you'll probably end up with some very bad choices, but they will be weeded as time moves on. Sticking to one color may help give some sort of unity to the collection. Over the years, I've found this to be very useful as I phase some out and bring in new ones.

✦ If you feel unsure, do keep things consistent: different shapes and sizes in the same material; consistent color will make things easier for you in designing what goes into the pots.

Start with the assumption that if you have a large enough pot or container—anything more than 18 inches in width—the right light conditions and good drainage, you can grow just about anything. Keep in mind that you are creating a landscape in miniature and all the principles of good design apply, especially the basic factors of scale and harmony.

The wonderful thing about containers is that you can move them around and reconfigure your planting designs all year round. I pot up invasive plants that would destroy this garden simply to have the pleasure of their company. You can bring pots indoors in the winter (it's surprising how long some annuals will last inside with the right treatment); or keep a collection as another element of hard design in the garden. One of the most enchanting displays I've seen is a stone bench with a series of old (or made to look old) terracotta pots arranged in a charming way beneath the bench. About six little ones became almost a freeform sculpture.

Container gardening will help anyone with a disability or who's in a wheelchair. Since the pots can be put on risers, they can be grouped for easy access. With plants jammed close together, a miniature universe can be arranged with lots of different plant types to work with, few weeds and plenty of versatility. To stabilize the pots, set on garden benches; or put a pot upside down, and use a pot of the same size right side up (this looks sculptural as well); or set pots on old bricks, and use a rod through the drainage holes.

Containers have many virtues, not the least being that you automatically have a raised bed, which means the soil warms up early and stays that way longer; it also never gets compacted. Diseases don't carry over from one season to the next, since you are constantly renewing the soil. You can plant intensively; in fact, it's important to do so. This will help to protect the soil and, surprisingly, keeps it moist. You won't have to deal with weeds, because there simply won't be enough room for them to grow.

Weather affects pots just as it does gardeners. When it gets too hot for you to be out in the sun, it's too hot for pots. Move them into a bit of shade; add some mulch to the surface so that moisture won't evaporate quickly.

Placing Containers

Many sensibilities come into play here. Obvious things, such as large pots with trees and shrubs to the rear and small ones to the foreground, come to mind. I like the idea of massing pots rather than having them dotted about the landscape. You can group pots so that they are the focal point in a small garden. You can also use them to frame a specific feature: stairways, a bench or a garden chair.

As my own pot collection has grown over the years, I find it very useful and convenient to have containers generous enough to hold a large plant at the ready to fill in potential holes left by perennials that have passed their best moments. You can set them into the border until some new flush of color comes along to please. I like to move other containers around when new color needs to be added or when a hole appears in my planting design from where I sit on the deck.

✦ Wall containers: They're tricky things, mainly because you've got to water them at least twice a day. You can, however, decorate a whole wall and fill only a few of them with actual plants. Most wall brackets look gorgeous filled with mosses or some of the larger sedums.

Hanging Baskets

The first rule to remember is that hanging baskets can be very heavy once filled and watered. Make sure they are anchored to a ceiling or wall with a very strong holder and placed so that they are easy to water. They will need daily attention, since drying out is fairly rapid.

Wire baskets, which look extremely handsome, must be lined with any of the following: sphagnum moss (the most common) or loose fibers such as coconut fiber, natural fibers or synthetic fibers specially designed for this job. If you use plastic as a liner, be sure there are drainage holes in the bottom. The easiest thing to do is get a preform basket that already has an aluminum pie plate to act as a water reservoir.

✦ Start by soaking the basket for about 15 minutes then let it drip until spongy.
✦ Set the basket in a pot large enough to stabilize it while you work. Let the segments of the liner overlap, and make holes where you want the plants to come through. Add a soilless potting mixture with added slow-release fertilizer, and fill to halfway without compacting the mixture.

There are a number of methods to get the plants into the basket. Try the following:

✦ Plant from outside, and push roots through by rolling the seedling in a newspaper (fish-and-chips style). Pull it through from inside so the leaves and stems protrude but roots remain in the mix, then remove paper.
✦ Put in clingers first (the plants that will cling to the moss around the basket), and make holes big enough to push the roots through so they touch the soil but don't get lost in the sphagnum, then close the hole up around the neck of the plant. Fill the pot with soil, and include a slow-release fertilizer.

3

Joanna Stein designed this entrance garden for Toto Soegandi. In an area 7 by 7 feet, she installed a fountain, a miniature box hedge, ornamental grasses and seasonal perennials. A hedge in front of the window disguises garbage cans and gives privacy. See page 74.

4

Temma Gentles and Victor Levin had this pocket garden installed right next to Temma's parking pad. The ornamental grasses can withstand the pollution from the car and the small planting looks good all year long. See pages 75 and 166.

✦ Add trailing plants to disguise the basket. Gently work the roots into the side of the basket, and then add a layer of soilless mix. When you reach the top, make sure there's at least 2 inches of soil between the trailing plants and those in the center. The final level of both soil and plants should be just at the basket's rim.

✦ Put the tallest plants in the center, and work toward the outside.

✦ At this stage, I'd put the basket in place simply because it's going to be a lot lighter and easier to hang than when it's soggy. Once in place, give it a good soak and let water drain out.

   Put hanging baskets in a place where the draining water won't fall on someone's head. In fact, heavy planters should never be placed over areas where there is any traffic. I don't care how stable a hanging basket may seem, I wouldn't want to run the risk of an accident.

✦ Place hanging baskets in a bright place, out of the wind for a couple of weeks so that roots can establish themselves in peace and when the risk of early-spring weather turning rotten is pretty much over.

✦ Pinch back the clingers so they will be bushier and get a chance to do the clinging—it's the new foliage that clings, not the old.

✦ Use foliage plants as a background or as fillers to give structure to a container arrangement.

Types of Container Materials

The most popular is terra-cotta, which is vulnerable to decay in colder areas and must be stored during periods of prolonged freeze-thaw cycles. They are made from clay, fired in a kiln and can be anything from giant mass-produced objects to one-of-a-kind works of art.

✦ Mass-produced types lend themselves to judicious painting: lead-gray, French blue, even stripes or deep, almost black-green.

✦ To make any terra-cotta pot look aged, paint with a combination of acidophilus yogurt and beer. This will form a base for moss to grow in and make them look ancient in no time at all.

✦ Fiberglass containers and window boxes are becoming increasingly popular, because they are made using the old molds and are astoundingly cheap. If you paint them in black-green or black, they look almost like the real thing for a fraction of the price.

✦ Stone: Among my favorites. If they are properly cleaned out in fall, stone pots will bear up under winter weather without serious cracking. They should blend in with the type of stone you are using in other parts of the garden (the patio, edging for borders, raised beds).

✦ Cast concrete: A substitute for stone. Thousands of these things are now being produced from ancient molds. They look okay, but are not a patch on the real thing. They are, however, extremely tough and can be left outside.

✦ Metal: I like using old copper troughs to stand containers in. I've tried filling them with stones and packing popcorn, but it's still much too heavy and a pain to take apart in winter. Now I put pots upside down in the bottom and stand other pots the right way up. It's easy to change the design of the planting and very easy to disassemble in fall.

✦ Galvanized buckets and, of course, if you can afford it, antique lead troughs or cisterns make good containers. Some of the new ones from Asia look incredible and aren't outrageously expensive.

✦ Verdigris: Get a verdigris kit and turn a prettily shaped bucket into something special. To do it yourself: Paint it up with a metal primer. Allow to dry, and then apply a base coat of acrylic paint in deep green or the basic color you want. Then, with a stippling brush, dab on contrasting or harmonizing shades of lighter and darker green over the whole surface; repeat with a second shade. Seal with a coat of acrylic varnish. All this should be done outside, because acrylic paints are toxic.

✦ Wood: Always looks classy, especially if you have a classic design like a Versailles tub. Placed on casters, they'll be easy to move around just as they did at Versailles.

✦ Plastic: Not ones I would choose unless out of absolute necessity. But if you have no choice because of budget or weight restrictions, by all means use these pots that are faked up to look like the real thing. Make sure they fade away to almost nothingness by painting them deep green, slate or pale, pale blue. That way, they won't call attention to themselves.

Interesting Objects as Containers

You can use almost anything for a planter. Habits come and go. The first time I saw an abandoned shoe filled with impatiens, I thought it was charming. The tenth time, not so. I wouldn't be bothered now. But if you do look around your house for things that you hate to throw out and would love to recycle, turn them into containers for plants. Just make sure that you'll be able to convert your *objet trouvé* into a proper plant holder with a drainage hole. You can drill a hole in the bottom or, if the container is malleable, heat up a nail on a candle and melt a hole in the bottom.

I've got the pieces of a shattered, rather large container scattered about the garden. I shove about a third of a chunk (they are generous sizes) into the ground and then plant behind it. Though not officially a pot, it looks like one.

✦ Try almost any metal container as a planter, from old bean pots to large tin ewers to a clothes trunk. Make sure it looks right rather than just a cute

source of conversation. If it doesn't fit with the overall design of the garden, give it away.

+ Scour junkyards, secondhand stores and lawn sales
  to find new sources of containers. Old toilets, cooking pots, mixing bowls, ancient sinks (metal or
  ceramic); weeping tiles or chimney pots come to
  mind as wonderful containers. An oil drum, a big
  plastic pot, a colander, even an abandoned sieve can
  all do good service. Nothing is too wild or too weird
  to be a container for plants. Just make sure the
  plants look right wherever you give them a home.

Container Maintenance

Cleaning pots regularly will not only help with the
health of the plant but prolong the life of the
container as well. This will also prevent bugs and
disease from carrying on their destructive work.

+ Use a firm scrub brush, and clean it thoroughly
  inside and out. Then wash with soap and warm
  water or a 1:5 bleach-and-water solution.
+ Soak terra-cotta pots before planting up. Clay
  absorbs lots of moisture and, if not presoaked, will
  take it from the growing medium.
+ Let wooden barrels sit in water until all the wood
  has swollen as much as it can. This will help make
  it watertight.
+ Keep containers off the ground. You can buy chocks
  (funny-looking little feet), or set them on bricks or

other pieces of wood. If I know I've got them in exactly the right place, I will set containers on flat pebbles. Just make sure the riser fits in with the design scheme. This is a must for wooden containers, since they will likely rot without air circulation.

Winter Protection

The bane of my life is getting the pots ready for winter. Some I leave planted up to come indoors; others simply have to be left outside in the toolshed. This little place is off the ground and in the lee of the house so that winter winds are at a minimum. These are two good principles to keep in mind when storing plants: off the ground and out of the wind.

+ If you have an unheated garage where pots can be left all winter in a frozen state, this is a great place for storage. Bring those with perennials out in April for a slow thawing-out, but don't let them get into a freeze-thaw state; pansies and primulas are the best and cheeriest plants for this time of year and the ones most likely to survive uncertain weather.
+ If you have a cool basement—one that stays around 50°F—and lights, you can maintain lots of plants that are right out of your zone and save money replacing the plants each year. Make sure there is adequate air circulation (I use an air cleaner); you need to have lights on for about 16 hours a day.

✦ Keep all plastic bubble wrap, and use it to wrap
fragile containers before stacking them up. Burlap
will do, as will layers of newspaper.

Moving Large Containers

Move large containers around to decide where you
want them before you plant up. But getting stuck with
a huge pot in the wrong place can happen to anyone.
Getting it to the right place is another matter. One of
those plastic snow carpets that kids use is ideal to keep
on hand for such jobs. Slide it under the pot, and have
someone very strong drag it to the right place.

✦ An easier method is always to have them on a riser
with rolling feet that lock into place. A flat square
of wood with casters will also be useful for moving
them around—as long as you have a hard, flat
surface to troll through.
✦ Use the old rollers and boards trick: Put two pieces
of board under the pot, shove two rollers (bits of
pipe or pole) under the board, and keep rolling it
along, adding the pipe to the front of the board.

When to Plant a Container

Planting up, repotting or potting on: You can tell
when a plant needs repotting, because it will appear to
be under serious stress (no amount of watering and
fertilizing will perk it up) or it may be pot-bound (just
pull it out of the pot, and it will be obvious).

✦ To increase growth: Shake the plant out of the pot, loosen the roots gently with your fingertips, being careful of the fine feeder roots. Repot in a size about 2 inches wider than the rootball, and use a fresh medium. Throw the old soil into the compost pile.

✦ Make sure you don't overpot when you change sizes. Go up only one or two sizes, and keep them planted closely.

✦ To reduce growth: Cut away about one-third of the main root with clean, sharp secateurs. Repot in a same-sized container.

✦ Planting bulbs: Calculate about six months in advance of flowering for spring bulbs, or three months for summer bulbs. Plant spring-flowering bulbs in autumn, summer-flowering bulbs in winter or spring.

✦ Tulips are particularly vulnerable to squirrel attacks where I live, and spring without tulips would be awful. Pots are one answer (there are few others). They can be filled with bulbs and put into place covered with mesh or chicken wire until sprouting.

✦ Perennials can be planted in either spring or summer, depending on the size of the pot (the bigger the better). So can conifers.

✦ Spring-flowering shrubs and trees (including broad-leaved evergreens) should be planted in autumn.

✦ Summer- and autumn-flowering shrubs and trees (including broad-leaved evergreens) should be planted in spring.

✦ Install water plants in late spring.

How to Plant a Container

By using clean pots (and drainage material) and fresh potting mixtures, you can go a long way to growing healthy plants. Regular watering, rather than ignoring them for long periods and then drowning the poor things, also helps.

I've used every method known to humankind in making suitable drainage, especially in large containers —from marbles to stone chips to broken pots to packing popcorn. Forget it. Make sure there's a drainage hole in the bottom, cover it with a piece of broken clay, and fill up with your planting mixture. It works as well as anything else and creates little fuss.

If you don't feel this is enough to keep soil from leaching out, add more shards from broken containers, a layer of horticultural cloth, pebbles or anything that will be easy to shake out of the pot. Packing popcorn, though light, is a pain in the neck to get out, and it's not something you can simply throw into the compost at the end of the season. Frankly, it's just not worth picking all this stuff out of the soil.

✦ If you have a valuable container *sans* drainage hole, put a stone or brick in the bottom, then plant up a container one size smaller, put it inside and continue as usual.

✦ Rule of thumb: Choose a container that's at least 2 inches larger than the rootball of the plant or plants to go inside.

The Soil Mix

Soil is just as important in container planting as in any other kind of gardening.

The mix is terrifically important. Don't think you can nip out into the garden and dig up some of that fine, black loam you have back there. It's too heavy, for one thing, and doesn't have the rapid-draining qualities that container plantings need. You can buy perfectly adequate soilless mixes containing vermiculite (holds in water) and perlite (provides aeration) at a garden center. But you can also experiment with your own mix, and here are a couple:

✦ Make an even mix of vermiculite or perlite and sand (builder's sand); use one third of this mixture and then add one third each of topsoil and compost. If you are using your own and not a commercial compost or topsoil that's been sterilized so that it's weed- and disease-free, put it in the oven at 160°F for about an hour. It smells up the place, but not enough to be discouraging. Just remember it's in there, and don't turn up the oven to preheat something for dinner. I can assure you the smell is quite revolting.

✦ The soilless mixes have few nutrients, so I always add some of my own compost to this mix, along with a bit of good garden soil (which I cheat and buy). You need something like this, especially for large containers, because you don't want to be emptying them completely every year.

✦ I use only compost of my own making for vegetables —I know there are no chemicals lurking about. Coarse sand can be added for drainage if you have heavy soil.

This is from *Organic Gardening* magazine and will give you an idea of how heavy soil can be. One cubic foot of soil weighs 50 to 90 pounds; i.e., 2 feet by 2 feet by 1 foot weighs between 200 and 300 pounds. Take this into account if you are planting on a deck or rooftop.

Watering

✦ Hold off soaking the new plants, and let them develop good root systems. The bigger they get, the more water they'll need, right up to once or twice a day when they are in full flush.

✦ Use large pans under containers, layer with pebbles, and fill with water. You can leave a pot for a couple of days this way.

✦ The Wick System: Commercial wick watering systems work very well, but you can make your own by twisting or braiding shoelaces or strips of old T-shirts cut into lengths. Bury one end in the pot, and put the other end in the bottom of a deep pail of water.

PROBLEMS

I never use chemicals in my garden, but if you do, be sure to read the instructions very carefully. Many plant deaths can be attributed to careless applications of these toxic poisons. You should apply them only on a windless day after sunset, or they'll be floating all over you, your kids, pets, beneficial bugs and the neighborhood. Frankly, when you have to be this careful, why run the risk?

Bugs

If you live higher than the seventh floor of an apartment building, you won't be getting the visitors the rest of us do. But you may be bringing bugs in on new plants. These are a few that will attack pot plants:

✦ Aphids: You'll see these hateful creatures marching lockstep up the side of a plant looking innocent enough, but they are sucking the life out of the plant. Even worse, the next generation will have wings and move on to other plants. Use a stiff spray of water (if you can bring the pot into the shower, this is a good start), nicking them off with Q-tips dipped in rubbing alcohol or a pint of water with a teaspoon of soap and a teaspoon of vegetable oil added. The best solution is to plant for lady bugs who will devour them with relish. Try installing Queen Anne's lace, nasturtiums, angelica, goldenrod, yarrow and evergreen euonymus.

✦ Slugs: Amazing creatures that will travel up the side of a relatively large pot overnight, nestle in and chomp anything with large, luscious leaves. If the container is large enough, put in a dish of water with sweetener or beer, and they'll fall in and drown.

Diseases

✦ Leaf spot: When spots with yellow edges appear on the leaves, pick them off; make sure you don't get leaves wet.

✦ Black spot: Spray with a garlic infusion (see Chapter 2).

✦ Downy mildew: White, downy growth. Remove leaves, make sure the ventilation is good, and spray with a mix of water and Epsom salts, 1 tablespoon:1 quart of water.

✦ Powdery mildew: A powderlike substance on the underside of leaves that causes them to yellow. Pick them off, and spray with a fungicide.

What to Plant

I have to start off any season planting as many *Helichrysum petiolare* as possible. This silvery, felted foliage plant is the most versatile there is. It's impossible to have too much. These are followed by the perennials I love in pots. If I have to use them as annuals, I don't mind that either.

Perennials

There are many perennials that lend themselves to container planting. Don't get trapped into the idea that you can use only annuals in pots. Be really adventurous. In big pots, for instance, almost any perennials will do beautifully (see "Winter Protection" page 54). At the top of the list are hostas, which can be a great addition to a shady corner along with ferns.

Grasses

I like to choose unusual-looking grasses to put in pots by themselves. Take *Ophiopogon planiscapus* 'Nigrescens.' Called black mondo grass, it is really black and needs a pale background to show it off; otherwise, it gets lost. *Hakonechloa macra* 'Aureola,' a brilliant yellow grass, combines beautifully with anything burgundy. It's also splendid in a pot. It tolerates shade, so looks good in dark corners. Try a bright blue fescue, *Festuca glauca*; or many of the bronze grasses, which look better in pots than in the ground to my eye.

Ferns

I adore ferns of all sorts, and a few pots of fronds will transform any dank, miserable corner into a thing of beauty. You can dig up that familiar bracken that seems to grow wild in every city garden or edge of a forest and put it into pots to fill a gloomy nook. Or consider Christmas fern, *Polystichum acrostichoides,* which is also evergreen. Put it in a frost-proof container to stay out all winter where it can be viewed through a convenient window.

Sedums and Sempervivums

You've got to have sedums, especially in shallow containers. The sempervivums, fondly known as hens-and-chicks or just semps, will crawl all over the surface of a stone or concrete container or trough. If you keep them over winter, place in a spot protected from both wind and moisture. Mine survive under the shelter of a table on the deck.

Sedum spathulifolium 'Purpureum,' a great favorite, is a lovely spreader and doesn't get too high. Just make sure that sedums have good drainage. See Chapter 11 for more sedums.

Without knowing it, I became a modest collector of sempervivums. At first, you may think they all look alike, but you couldn't be more wrong. They have huge variations and many subtle leaf forms and edgings. I prefer to see them in pots by themselves, but that's because I like looking at them *en famille.* Just a personal prejudice here.

Vines

I love container-grown vines; here are some useful, sun-loving ones:

✦ Clematis species such as *C. texensis, C. alpina* and many of the early-flowering cultivars will need a 12-inch pot. Get a bushy, compact plant. Clematis won't take well to plastic; pot them up in terra-cotta so the root system will be protected from hot summer weather. It seems difficult to prune clematis hard once you've planted it the first year, but it will become such a strong plant down the road, just grit your teeth and get on with it. After that, do normal pruning in March or April, and train the vine up a support.

✦ *Ipomoea batatas* 'Blackie' is in the moonflower family but has a deep purple-black foliage and looks strange and interesting when it's used properly—hanging over the edge of a pot or climbing a wall.

✦ *Plectranthus argentatus* is a beauteous, silver foliage plant with mauve flowers. There are now other versions of this great plant (see Chapter 11).

Invasives

Containers are the ideal place for the wonderful, invasive plants that would take over and destroy a pocket garden. Just a few suggestions that are rather special:

✦ Pineapple mint, *Mentha suaveolens,* is light green with cream edging.

✦ Blue lyme grass, *Elymus glaucus.* I would never put this anywhere but in a big container, preferably a

5

Liz Knowles' small formal herb garden.
See page 76 for a description.

6

Barbara Sears planted her front garden most imaginatively. The Japanese maple, *Acer palmatum*, is placed perfectly within the planting. See pages 77 and 80.

huge tin pot plunged into the ground. This is a great-looking plant but unbelievably aggressive.

✦ Variegated goutweed, *Aegopodium podagraria* 'Variegatum,' is about the most invasive plant there is. Alas, it's very attractive with pale green leaves outlined in white, which would brighten up any shady corner. But it's a killer, and there's the real problem. It will choke out everything else in the garden. Ah, but put it in a big pot in a shady corner, and you've got a good plant. Please don't use it in any other way.

Shade Lovers

✦ Good clingers include creeping zinnia, *Sanvitalia procumbens*; Swan River daisy, *Brachycome*; creeping Jenny, *Lysimachia nummularia* 'Aurea' or *L. congestifolia* 'Outback Sunset,' with lemon-yellow flowers and golden-green foliage; and all of the lamiums.

✦ Trailers for the shade: Golden creeping daisy, *Wedelia trilobata*; *Nemesia* 'Innocence' (white), 'Confetti' (light mauve pink) and 'Joan Wilder' (deep pink); creeping snapdragons with silver foliage and white flowers; *Convolvulus* 'Morning Trails' (pale blue); *Mimulus aurantiacus*, in a lovely soft apricot.

Container Combinations

Here are some other unusual ideas for container plantings:

+ *Corydalis flexuosa* 'Blue Panda'; cherry-pie heliotrope, *Heliotropium peruvianum*; baby blue eyes, *Nemophila menziesii*; begonias; and lobelia.

+ Let groundcovers, such as lamiums and creeping Jenny, *Lysimachia nummularia*, and trailing petunias hang over the edges of pots.

+ Try annuals such as petunias, lobelia and bacopa with a trailing potato vine, *Solanum jasminoides.*

+ Fill a large container with a combination of succulentlike plants such as sedums, sempervivums and annual echeverias.

+ Put together a wild purple petunia like 'Purple Wave' with orange and yellow mimulus and corncockle.

+ Trailing viola, *Viola hederacea*, with rhodochiton, lobelia and lamiums.

+ Trailing *Helichrysum petiolare*, fuchsias, scaevola, impatiens and geraniums.

Vegetable Gardening in Containers

Container-grown vegetables are a dandy way to save space or for a balcony or deck or where you have only a small sun spot. And that spot is important. Vegetables need at least six hours of sun; many need even more. If you have too much shade, try some root vegetables (carrots and radishes); in a searing or very hot site, eggplants and cantaloupe will thrive.

With six hours of sun, it's possible to grow all the wonderful Mediterranean herbs so aromatic and wonderful in cooking: oregano, rosemary, marjoram, parsley. Herbs and vegetables require at least 6 inches of soil to thrive. To grow them, try at least a 13-inch pot.

I've seen marvelous half-barrel vegetable gardens that hold stalks of corn, tomatoes and peppers. Set on rollers or a moveable dolly, half-barrels or large pots can be moved about to cash in on available sunny areas.

Here are some tips for vegetable gardening in containers:

✦ Put tomatoes and peppers in the center up against wire cages; then surround them with annual herbs such as basils (different kinds and colors).

✦ For a pretty container vegetable garden use a clean bushel basket lined in plastic with holes for drainage and then jam it with vegetables and herbs.

✦ Everyone should have a pot of chives; mint should be planted only in a container because it's so invasive; rosemary has to be brought indoors in winter, but sage can stay outdoors in a large enough container.

✦ Potatoes look good and surprisingly ornamental, as do beets when grown in a large basket.

✦ Combine different kinds of tomatoes: my favorites are 'Sweet 100' or 'Sweet Million,' which produce enormous numbers of cherry tomatoes and take up little room. And there's always good old 'Tiny Tim' for value.

✦ Save space and grow your plants upward. Beans, tomatoes, cucumbers, even squash and peppers will grow up quite happily. Lash bamboo stakes together to form a trellis. Or drive three stakes into the container as far as possible, then string wire (I use fishing wire, which is invisible and indestructible) in a design that's pleasing to your eye.

✦ You can easily make a tepee of bamboo stakes.

✦ I like to use lengths of hardware cloth. This is a metal mesh that comes in different sizes of openings, from tiny ($1/4$ inch) to large (2 inch), and are easily cut to the right size. They can be supported by a wall or trellis or wooden frame with L-shaped hooks.

✦ Use cylindrical tomato cages, and fix them into the planter securing the top to a wall so the wind won't blow it over.

✦ Container sizes: Lettuce and chives need 6-inch pots but will do better in one 10-inch. Peppers and tomatoes: 12-inch diameter, or a 5-gallon pot about 15 inches across.

✦ Here's an idea from *Organic Gardening*: Chop up all the plants in the autumn, mix them with the soil in containers along with straw mulch, then add a 4-inch layer of straw. Water and stir the pots, and they'll be ready to replant in spring.

Problems

✦ Nitrogen deficiency: The entire plant looks pale; old leaves go yellow.

◆ Potassium deficiency: Old leaves are very pale; new growth looks normal.

Starting Seeds in Containers

Given such a small amount of space and the number of seeds in a packet, you can save money by sharing with a hortbuddy. Just get a seedling or two of your favorites, or sow the following directly from seed: beans, beets, carrots, cucumbers, lettuce, Swiss chard, spinach and, of course, tomatoes.

◆ Any annual herb, such as basil, dill or coriander, also takes well to this treatment.

4

Front Yards

What a nightmare a front yard can be. Here's your image plastered for all the world to see; here's the statement of how much you care about your neighborhood; and, most important, here is the entrance to your home. In real estate, they call what you see "curb appeal." In landscape architecture, it's part of the streetscape. How do you stack up?

A little history here is warranted. In North America, we've developed a tradition, call it landscape vernacular, of having grass, at least one specimen plant and a few foundation plantings. Street visible from the house, house visible from the street. This has led to a consistent, bland landscape from street to street, overseen by large trees.

I find it discouraging to wander through some of our suburbs and see nothing but the usual, pointy evergreen at the edge of the house, a few mounded types in front of the bow window and acres of grass.

To me, that's not gardening—that's green wallpaper. It's empty space that could be filled up with trees and shrubs giving habitat to birds, insects and animals. And what pleasure to the eyes.

The next cliché is the poor, benighted Japanese maple stuck in the middle of what one ecologist calls green cement. Or, in our region, the ubiquitous forsythia or bridalwreath spirea, which look glorious in spring and boring for the rest of the year.

It's a radically changing vision as more people of all ages get involved with gardening. They are finding the need to have a real front garden increasingly important—a pocket garden to the rescue. The front yard, no matter how minute, can be a great entrance. It can disguise or distract the eye from a boring bit of architecture. It can be fun to work in. It's a grand way to meet the neighbors. And, once again, scale and simplicity are the key to making an amiable entrance to the house.

If you live in a condominium or townhouse or the inner city, don't be intimidated by a handkerchief-sized patch of ground and feel there's nothing to be done with it. I've watched this change take place since I turned my front yard into a garden. There seems to be an invisible line that's crossed when guests come onto our property. They view it almost as though it is part of the house. I watch people come up the short walk and slow down to look at the small garden beside it. It gives me pause to get myself ready and reach the door to welcome them. All in the space of a few feet.

Most people, unless they're moving into a new house, tend to leave the front garden until last. I did, and it wasn't until I started working there that I really got involved with my neighbors. It was because of our chats over our front gardens that the street formed an ecology group with its attendant impact on the health and survival of birds and bees in the neighborhood. No matter where or how you garden, there is some sort of repercussion.

The hideous habit developers have of putting garages in the most prominent part of any suburban garden has downgraded this important part of the garden, allowing the car once again to take precedence over people. But newer developments are cutting out this egregious habit, putting cars behind houses or providing alleys for parking.

Begin with the style of your house. The entrance to it really starts at the street. Scale becomes singularly important here. Unless you've got a professional designer who's worked out a clever solution, having a pretentious gate leading up to a tiny cottage just might not work very well at all.

Proximity to the street will dictate much of what you can do. Pollution is a serious hazard to any front garden. If salty snow is dumped all over your front garden, you've got to work with solid material and plants that will be able to tolerate this. Or get out and shovel the minute the snow lands.

See Joanna Stein's imaginative solution in Toto Soegandi's garden (shot #3) for the smallest proper front garden we could find. It measures only 7 feet by 7 feet, yet it contains ornamental grasses, a minuscule boxwood hedge around an oversized (for the space) fountain and seasonal perennials; there's also a fine bit of stonework to make easy access to the house from front or side. It's a brilliant solution to the front garden, requiring almost no care and little upkeep except to keep weeds from between the stones.

Any space can be a garden, but there are a few principles to keep in mind before you do anything in front of your house.

+ Decide whether you are making a garden for use or strictly for enhancement of the house. If you want to be able to use the garden for sitting or even to entertain in, you will have to make some pretty interesting screens and fencing. Otherwise, it's complete exposure to the street.

+ You can have built-in sitting spaces, even in a pocket-sized garden. Plan a seating area surrounded by enough plants to give at least a semblance of privacy. Sometimes, the front garden has the best light at the end of the day, just when you want to have a nice, cool drink.

+ Don't plant trees and shrubs so that they will bonk someone on the head or side of the face or provide a potential hiding place for burglars. I hate to think about this, but we've had stuff stolen from the front that was practically anchored in place (trucks out shopping for nice ornaments, no doubt with a client in mind.)

✦ If you must accommodate a car in the front of your house, look at Temma Gentles' front garden (see shot #4). This is a pocket planting next to her parking pad. The plants are all tough; they can withstand both the salt from the street as well as the exhaust from the car every time it starts. Keep this firmly in mind when choosing plants.

✦ Take into consideration what's already there and what you have no control over. The inevitable city-owned street tree is sacrosanct. In our area, we are stuck with silver maples—huge forest trees with the shallowest of feeder roots. Magnificent in the forest, hell in the city. My solution to this was to raise the beds under the tree and fill it with as many plants as the space would hold. It's a constant battle to keep everything fed. And the tree looks alarmingly healthy.

✦ Check the scale of the plants. Low clumps will make it appear that you're working with a much larger space. Miniature conifers, dwarf birch, or Japanese maples in a group can make a rich statement and create a dense planting that doesn't require a great deal of work.

✦ I've created a checkerboard pattern in my own backyard to emphasize the narrowness of the garden (19 feet) but also to make planting pockets for any number of plants that love to have their roots under the warmth of stone. You can install dozens of herbs, such as sage, lavender and thyme, in such conditions. This idea could easily be translated on a small scale to an entrance garden.

✦ I love the idea of having huge pots as an entrance to a house. Not only are they very welcoming, but you have an enormous flexibility in palette and a medium where you can change your mind as well as plants with the seasons. But you have to make sure they are secure if you live in a place where safety is a factor.

✦ In a super-small space, don't futz around with curves that mean nothing. A straight path to the front door works best. Concentrate on the planting nearby to be the big attraction.

✦ If the light conditions are right, think about a herb garden such as the one Liz Knowles has in her garden (see shot#5). This design can be translated into almost any condition, provided you have the right kind of pot for the center and a few nice old bricks. In this case, each quadrant is treated individually, and each has a strong planting plan that works in harmony with the next. It never appears to be out of control. Artemisias, sages, thymes, lavender, small ornamental grasses, Russian sage, *Perovskia* and santolina are all wonderfully drought-tolerant. Then a New Zealand phormium is added here for central focus.

✦ Barbara Sears' north-facing garden (see shot #6): Now this is the way to use a Japanese maple in front of the house—as part of the whole border.

✦ Make hedges of boxwood or artemisia (*A. camphorata* is superb but requires regular pruning). A boxwood-lined walk can make a strong entranceway, but don't back it with straggly plants. Keep the area behind planted with low groundcovers, herbs or dwarf roses.

✦ Keeping out the dog (or child) from hell: Plant things with definite spikiness, such as *Acanthopanax sieboldianus,* or structural plants such as Adam's needle, *Yucca filamentosa.*

Make sure you are keeping your own view in mind when you install the front garden. Your view of it is as important if not more so than what the garden looks like from the street. Don't put anything large in front of windows. Let the light shine in, and avoid having to prune constantly. I look over a small front garden that's designed almost like a tapestry. But over the years, this got boring. The tapestry is now a background for ornamental grasses, small shrubs and other, more vertical plants. Having a good combination of the two will make you happiest.

Tips for Maintaining a Front Garden

✦ If you've installed bricks or flagstones and don't want weeds to pop up between them, pour boiling water over the plants before they have a chance to set seed. Allow plants such as mosses or false mosses such as sagina to grow in their place.

✦ Let leaves lie where they fall. They will be scooped up by worms eventually and they do provide a form of mulch for the garden.

✦ Figure out what you're going to do with the garbage cans. They are unsightly and inconvenient. A square lattice barrier covered with vines can be very effective. Make sure you have easy access to the containers both in summer and winter.

✦ Don't let plants grow willy-nilly. Always plan on pruning in spring and fall and nip back anytime for tidiness.

Formal Style

✦ Arrow-straight paths lined with boxwood or some other hedging.

✦ A patio and broad paths with raised beds can create the feeling of formality, if needed.

Informal Style

✦ Have low-growing plants, but always include a few larger ones to give the garden some contrast.

✦ Combine plants with similar foliage so your planting doesn't look too wild.

✦ Use unusual edgers such as coral bells, *Heuchera*. These plants are handsome, come in a variety of foliage colors, from magenta to pink to dull pewter, and require little care (see page 194).

✦ Instead of Japanese maple, use dwarf birch, *Betula nana*, or a star magnolia, *Magnolia stellata*, but don't leave them all alone. Surround them with low-growing groundcovers and have a stepping-stone walk through the space.

Driveways

Surely the biggest pain of all, usually the most unattractive and most highly used. Here's such a functional part of your yard, something that must be shoveled and kept in good condition and is probably an eyesore. My instinct, driven by a thirst for more plants, would be to turn the garage into a storage and seating area, rip out the driveway and turn it into garden. The car can be left to the street or stored somewhere else. But then, I don't drive.

Design Tips for the Pocket Front Garden

You'll notice, no doubt, that I slip from saying "yard" to "garden" the minute I've made a suggestion about adding plants. This is both unconscious and conscious. It seems that a garden can be created with the simplest of all elements: one good plant placed just so. You often see this in Europe. Flowers and color will be confined to pots, and there will be one perfect tree or shrub to grab all the rest of the interest.

✦ Unity is a large part of all good design. If you harmonize the structure of your front garden with the house, it will give you clues on how you should approach the driveway.

✦ If you look at Barbara Sears' front garden again (see shot #6), you'll see how effective a dense planting can be that follows a strict order of large at the rear (the cedar) to small edgers at the front. Taking out pavers on a jagged pattern gives the feeling of plenitude here. The Japanese maple is nicely integrated with groundcovering plants and small mounded forms such as *Artemisia schmidtiana* 'Silver Mound' that echo its shape so pleasingly.

✦ A front-yard garage can be perked up no end by making it into a painting. I don't mean putting a phony landscape scene on it; I mean painting it in colors that will give true eye appeal. One of the most dazzling I've ever seen had double-panel doors. The inside panels are painted bright green outlined in blue; the outside panel, a bright green. Huge pots anchored into place flanked the door and were filled with harmonizing annuals spilling out and softening the edges. Naturally, a solution like this has to go with the house and certainly isn't for the faint of heart.

✦ Paint first, then cover a garage with vines. If the garage doesn't have any architectural features that tie it into the house, you can always retrofit them. Grape, wisteria, Boston ivy, Virginia creeper and climbing

7

Larry Davidson designed this pocket garden mainly to use up the gorgeous old bricks he had on hand. The pattern immediately draws the eye while the selection of plants insinuates itself subtly. See page 92.

8

Jan Sugarman's back yard is a
model pocket garden. See page 94
for a description of the plants.

hydrangea will, after a few years, make a complete cover. The supporting structure should be in good condition. Vines can get very heavy over the years and you don't want them pulling anything down.

✦ Even if you can't afford to have ancient cobblestones, use a contrasting and attractive brick to edge the driveway and make it less ugly.

✦ Raised beds on either side of the driveway make it possible to cram in plants that spill over but won't get bruised by the movement of the car. Make sure that some have winter interest—cotoneaster or blue oat grass, *Helictotrichon sempervirens,* for instance.

✦ One of the most attractive approaches I've seen was in England. The driveway was paved, but the center part where the tires never touched was planted with a low, groundcovering, mosslike evergreen plant such as *Sagina subulata.* I did a similar one that pleased me a great deal. The driveway was repaved with the center part removed and low-growing plants put in between (the edges were supported so that they didn't crumble with the weight). At the edges, a gravel garden was installed in slightly raised beds (see how to do this in Chapter 9). Tough, ornamental grasses were planted. The service area (garbage cans) was blocked off with simple trellising.

✦ Put low boxwood hedges on either side of the drive. This will block your view of the driveway and give it definition. Alongside the driveway is another good place to put trelliswork with lots of sturdy climbers. In one suburb I know, the designer tried putting up a fence to cut out the view of a particularly hideous driveway next door. The local bylaws cut him off. He then designed screens set at slight angles to each other and smothered them with vines. It looks great.

+ Make sure that you haven't blocked the sight of the street for when you back out of the driveway.

+ Create some sort of barrier between drive and house—for example, a fence with a gate to the entrance. To give a fence the feeling of luxe, add a mirror or well-fitted Mylar, cover with vines and tall perennials and add a small tree. You get to see the garden reflected back to the house and banish the driveway from sight.

+ Garbage cans can be installed in a shed with a removable front, making them easy to roll out to the curb.

+ Privacy from the street may be difficult with a handkerchief-sized front garden, but you can plant well-formed arching shrubs such as golden or variegated elder (birds love the fruit as well), which won't intrude on the street.

Lighting

Paths and the porch or house should be properly lit. It seems obvious, but that isn't always the case. You'd be surprised at how often they are obscured or guests made to feel as if they're going through a barrier. Being able to read a house number means good placement that can be seen from the road. If it can't be read clearly, get new numbers or change the positioning. Then make sure you use a strong enough light. Because of its size, you won't need a great deal of lighting in a pocket garden. But one well-placed outdoor lamp beneath a particularly handsome specimen plant will perk up the front garden at night and afford a certain amount of security as well.

Paths

A good link from the sidewalk to the entrance of the house says more about how you want to welcome people than anything else. We got together with our next-door neighbors (we're in a semi-detached) and made a common walk, then rejigged the stairs and painted both halves of the house the same color. It won't change the fact that these are dull houses architecturally, but it does give them some cohesion.

✦ Wide steps, which we share, also make it a welcoming place. They are perfect for sitting in the late-afternoon sun, talking to the kids or chatting with neighbors. It was the best investment both our families have made.

✦ In a pocket garden, there's no point in having anything except a straight path. Something with a little meander or twist isn't going to add much to small-garden design. And you might want to look around at what everyone else in the neighborhood is using if you are looking for some sort of mass style.

✦ Make sure the path gives you as much garden space as possible without cheating on the width. A narrow path can be an obstacle course for an older person or a child.

✦ Brick looks right with most older houses and can be laid out in a variety of attractive patterns. Fieldstone works with a large, less formal house. (See pages 7 and 92 for some good path solutions.)

✦ Any kind of low-growing plants will soften the edges of a dull path.

Porches

Our porch has always been the spot where we store stuff. We made a huge effort to make it neat and welcoming, but it's still a dump site. To counteract this, we have big pots of plants to distract the eye. The plants change seasonally, but there are enough perennials that there's always something interesting going on. Decorating in the winter becomes an easy task, and it's something to look out on when I work.

✦ Even the tiniest porch should be protected from the elements so you can get out a key or struggle with groceries. Pots of annuals plus some truly beautiful furniture would complete this scene.

✦ Plants should be in scale with the porch and the front door. A huge cedar blocking the view from indoors makes a gloomy sort of entrance.

Fencing

Avoid a fortress look: Solid fences appear forbidding; something more see-through gives definition but also offers a view through to the other side. A wooden fence with a small overhead framing the entry at the sidewalk can be effective, adding architectural interest and height. We have neighbors who put in a 7-foot fence the minute they moved in. We never got to know them, and years later, even when the fence was cut back to legal size, we knew what they thought of us. Fences can make or break neighborliness. When installing a new one, always get neighbors on-side to save problems down the road.

✦ A low metal (wrought iron, perhaps) fence always looks brilliant with a front pocket garden. The scale seems right. A boxwood hedge would also be appropriate. We've found it's hard to keep kids and dogs from running through the garden and either of these solutions might help. Unfortunately, highly prickly, thorned and pointed plants didn't deter them, either. What did work was masses and masses of plants. The message finally got through—keep out.

✦ Putting in a small stone fence dripping with plants would be an ideal but expensive solution. It's much easier to have a barrier with pots large enough to make sure they are permanent. You could also build raised planters all around the garden.

✦ Tall shrubs artfully pruned and underplanted with hostas can make a good barrier to the street. Serviceberry, *Amelanchier*, is one of my favorite screening plants—the airiness of the leaves, the meltingly beautiful blossoms in spring will make this a far better barrier than a fence, which might only emphasize how tiny a pocket the front garden really is.

5

The Back Garden

In theory, almost anything can become a pocket garden, but you'll find that the back garden is one of the most important places in the whole world. It's an extension of your house, a place for rest and recreation, an escape from the world. There is no other sanctuary quite as significant. Though a pocket garden by its very nature isn't going to be huge, you also don't want to feel claustrophobic when you are outside. Everything can close in on you in a city or town, from a nearby apartment building to just plain annoying neighbors. When we're under assault, gardening is meant to alleviate problems.

For these reasons alone, the pocket back garden means thinking through everything you've ever learned about gardening very carefully. And what's around is crucial. That awful garage, someone else's intrusive trees, the sight of a basketball hoop. There's always something in a town garden that's distracting.

You'll have to think of ways to block them out.

First of all, deal with reducing any chance of claustrophobia. You'll have to work on illusions of space and you can check the garden design chapter on that. Have vines all along the fences and higher where you want to use them as a vista. Do this by adding trelliswork to the top of fences, say at the end of the garden so that the eye is going to something dense.

Mirrors, forced perspective, fooling the eye with tricks all have an important place in a back garden. Raised beds at the end of a garden can also give that illusion of something climbing upward, ergo, a vista. Knocking down fences but leaving a privacy area is another trick that works well in our neighborhood. Having small moments echoed in each garden gives the feeling that things are much larger than they are in reality.

First, clean out the space so you can see what you have going for you. Borrowing a neighbor's view is always a good place to start. If they have a good tree that blooms profusely in spring, why put up something close by to compete with it?

Start with the bones of the garden. In most cases for pocket gardens, this is going to be with shrubs and small trees rather than a lot of construction. Get whatever pattern you want in your garden first. If it's to come from paving stones, gravel or a deck, make a choice early on in your plans and keep it consistent.

One of the best ways I've seen of pulling a small garden together is to have decking and furniture all of a piece: The decking consisted of fine wooden slats echoed in the design of the furniture. They looked as if they belonged together. You can start by finding a good piece of furniture and designing the deck around it. Conversely, build a good deck and find furniture that will enhance it.

Well-designed furniture in a small setting is a must. Having tacky stuff thrown in for no reason other than cheapness will be a glaring error. You'll be using this room a great deal once you've finished and it's a shame to stint on the furnishings. You'll also find that harsh, white furniture might prove to be too shrill in a very small setting. Dark, soft wood or metal painted black-green will last longer and look incredibly fresh for many years. The more you think of your back garden as a garden room, the more easily you'll be able to accommodate what you might originally think of as frills.

One small garden I found great delight in started with excellent furniture. Then all the forms and structure in the garden were designed to echo those shapes. The circle of the table became a motif throughout. The borders were semicircles around a small brick patio large enough to hold the table and chairs. A small pergola in the center divided the garden space (16 feet wide by 30 feet deep) into two distinct "rooms." Passing through the pergola (adorned with circles) gave the feeling of transition into another, very different space.

The plantings in the first room were heavy on lilies and roses, plus annuals. In the second, shadier room, there were muted woodland plants, a small seating area under a vine and a tiny fountain. The whole effect was one of great serenity, yet lush and sensual.

The Microclimate

Among the first things to consider is an analysis of your microclimate: how much sun hits each part of the garden; where does the prevailing wind land (this can make a big difference to where you plant shrubs); how much protection there is. If the howling north wind bangs right into your space, it's important to make a wind barrier. You can do this almost immediately by planting a row of trees such as cedar (see below) or screening shrubs such as serviceberry; or build high trelliswork covered with vines. The site will dictate how much it will be able to accommodate.

One of the major joys of a tiny backyard is just how many different varieties of plants you can grow. You won't be able to plant in huge drifts, but you can use a large number of different plants in an interesting palette with a variety of foliage textures. Biodiversity is truly the catchword for gardening in a small space. The more variety you have, the healthier an environment you'll make.

✦ Cedars as a windbreak are wonderful, but only if you have enough space—they are considered to be gross feeders, and it's hard to plant close to their base. You'd need at least 18 inches of space between the hedge and the plants you want to install (you might want to put a path next to them). If you have that much to spare, by all means, a cedar hedge makes an excellent background for plants and it is the best of all windbreaks.

✦ To have high, dappled shade, consider the following very hardy plants (check out Chapter 11 for further descriptions): serviceberry, *Amelanchier canadensis*; river birch, *Betula nigra*, is a native North American; elder, *Sambucus canadensis*; and redbud, *Cercis canadensis*.

✦ If you have dark shade from a nearby building, you will not be able to do anything except compensate. Good, humusy soil with lots of golden and variegated plants will brighten up what might become a murky, dank area. Hostas will grow in the most incredibly awful situation, but don't just settle for the ordinary ones; find the gorgeous little golden, blue and variegated forms to animate a dull area. There are so many good new cultivars of lungwort, *Pulmonaria saccharata*, you can almost become a collector. Named forms such as 'Peaches and Cream,' 'David Ward' and 'Roy Davidson' have wonderful, long graceful petals mottled with silver or pewter, with blooms that range from pink to blue. I can't recommend them highly enough. Then there's the good old deadnettle, *Lamium*; there isn't a garden that won't be perked up with this lovely old-fashioned plant.

✦ Figure out what you can do with the barbecue, tools

and equipment. If you don't have a garage, consider building a really efficient little tool house that fits in with the whole design of the garden. Even better, get the stuff out of the way, behind a trellis screen or at the side of the house.

Water in the Garden

What every back garden needs is the sound of water, so be sure to check below and in Chapter 10 for ideas on some easy, inexpensive ways to have a water feature.

Paths and Steps

Even a tiny garden needs a path to help define its spaces and how you want people to react to your garden. You can speed them up or slow them down with a path. A path can hide things or reveal them. A path is the difference between a yard and a garden. Lay a path, and you are making a major decision on where you'll go with your design.

Wood or bark chips, to my eye, look good only in a forest. I like the idea of lovely old bricks in simple patterns, like the one in Larry Davidson's garden (see shot #7). There are precast forms that look like old brick, and any local limestone or granite in blocks will make a graceful walk. Gravel, of course, is a great favorite and works well with old-fashioned plants.

✦ Choose a material that is restful and use it through-out. It's always a temptation to use wood, as well as stone and brick and so on. In a really tiny garden, consistency is a virtue.

✦ To set a path in place, choose a material designed for outdoor use. Many of the old bricks, unfortunately, are too soft for our polluted atmosphere.

✦ Planting between large stepping-stones will make them look as though they've been in place for years. Mosses look right in a woodland or shade garden; thymes in the bright light. Corsican mint looks good and isn't invasive, as are most of the other edible mints. Once again, I highly recommend Irish moss, *Sagina subulata*, which is not a moss at all but does have that look.

✦ And if you must have grass, make a grass path. Be sure that it's wide enough to accommodate a lawn mower for easy cutting.

✦ Steps up or down in even the smallest garden give it some contour and the illusion of more space. The merest suggestion of a change in elevation is always useful. But don't be mingy; make the steps wide enough for two people to walk down. Large stone slabs are the most satisfying, and since you won't have a huge flight of stairs, just one or two, it won't break the bank either.

✦ A terraced look: Use wooden risers backed by gravel steps. This can be expanded on either side into raised beds with the width of the steps determining how deep the terraces will be.

The Well-Designed Pocket Back Garden

As an example of a well-structured pocket back garden, we chose Jan Sugarman's. She has a tiny garden but a big soul and is as devoted a gardener as I've ever seen. Her garden (see shot #8) is 15 feet wide by 17 feet deep cut on an angle. It was begun in 1980.

Before she actually knew anything about gardening, she put in four shrubs, one for each season: a forsythia for spring, followed by a lilac, *Syringa*, then a PeeGee hydrangea, *Hydrangea paniculata* 'Grandiflora,' for a show all summer long, and a variegated dogwood, *Cornus*, for its leaf form and red bark in winter. Her instincts were perfect for a good start.

When the lilac died, she put in a Russian olive, *Elaeagnus angustifolia*. It's very brittle, and snow broke off the top branches a few years ago; it's just beginning to grow again. An emerald-green cedar beside it screens out a neighbor's unsightly garage, and just beyond, she installed a fence—a lattice one to let in light. This meant she could plant yellow roses (*Rosa* 'Golden Wings' and a David Austen yellow). When the family sit on the deck, they can't see the garage anymore but can see the vaulting roses in season.

Over the years, she found herself in a kind of dialectic with her garden. Every time she made a choice on one side of the garden, she had to do something with the other side for balance. When the grungy back shed was removed, it opened up the windows at the back of the house to the garden. A small deck and steps were added and they still had more garden space than the shed had allowed. Even though they don't own a car, the Sugarmans rent a garage to keep all their junk and tools in—it's no farther away than a garage would be on a normal estate, says Jan.

It quickly became apparent during the winter months that something was needed to counteract what she felt was the bitty quality of the yard. The more she looked out her windows, the more she found being able to view the garden was a real help in getting through the winter as well as planning for the future.

She wanted diversity of plants and stones. In contrast with the small size of the borders (10 by 3, sometimes 4, feet), they felt the strong need for homogeneous elements. And that was in the path they chose.

They started out with crazy paving set out just to get through the garden to tend plants. When the Sugarmans decided that something had to change, they knew they couldn't afford expensive stonework such as interlocking brick. The crazy paving, on the other hand, only underlined the lilliputian quality of the garden. In the end, they chose multicolored pea gravel as their solution. It was also evocative of Jan's childhood, when everyone in the 'burbs had gravel driveways. The sound of the crunch underfoot gives it another level of memory.

The path is 2 feet at its widest but narrows toward the back and curves slightly as though going off into a distant woodland. This is a brilliant move, because it really does fool the eye into thinking there is more space at the rear. As Jan points out, the narrowing of the path and bending it around the hydrangea draws the eye into and down the garden.

To carry on this illusion, she places pots at regular intervals along the edges of the path. The farther they get from the house, the smaller they are, adding to the sense of depth.

Once the underlying structure of shrubs and vines was created, she concentrated on seasonal perennials. Over time, she came to understand that she could have hundreds of plants and countless bulbs in bloom right through three seasons. She now has more than 80 different varieties of perennials, and dozens of shrubs, vines and trees. In spring, she starts with winter aconite, hepatica and bloodroot, and there's always something in bloom right up to the asters and mums in the autumn.

Jan kept variegated hostas under the hydrangea and added *Pulmonaria saccharata* 'Mrs. Moon,' *Fritillaria meleagris* and the late-blooming tulip, 'Spring Green.' She has a carpet of green, yellow and purple. There's also a much-prized *Hosta* 'Royal Standard,' which a friend gave her when she was on the prowl for *H. plantaginea grandiflora*, an old, hard-to-find species with wonderful-smelling flowers.

In late summer, there is a big contrast in a sunflower called 'Italian White.' Along the paths is the highly scented *Geranium macrorrhizum*, which imparts its pleasant odor every time it's touched. This makes working in the garden pure pleasure.

Then she places pots advantageously around: the gray, feathery foliage is *Lotus berthelotii*, a plant that, if it got enough sun, would have yellow flowers. Then there's a corner-store fuchsia called 'Thalia,' which has no protruding stamens and looks more refined than the familiar blowsier one. In front of it, she has Bowles golden grass, black pansies and lemon thyme. A coleus that echoes the orangey-red pink of the fuchsia is added for good measure.

The need for walls in the pocket garden was instantly recognizable to Jan Sugarman. She jammed in *Clematis virginiana* Virgin's bower, *C. macropetala* and five-leaf akebia, *Akebia quinata*, in one spot. Using the fence as walls, she added half a dozen other varieties of clematis and ivies. Another really good stroke is the hanging baskets connected to the fence among the vines. People pass by and then come up short for this little pocket of surprise.

And that's another of Jan's principles: having as many little surprises as possible even in this small space. For instance, on one fence, there's Boston ivy, *Parthenocissus tricuspidata*, and climbing hydrangea, *Hydrangea petiolaris*, with a pot of abutilon hanging from the fence between them. The abutilon has a tiered bloom that echoes the hydrangea. These little pockets, she says, become a whole world of exploding sensuality.

"In a tiny garden, there's such a special world, an exquisite botanical world. In a garden this small, you are always walking through beauty."

Follow Jan Sugarman's example:

◆ The crazy paving was moved to the side of the house, where it serves as risers for potted plants (see shot #8). This is an area that gets up to five hours of sun a day, even though it's in a side alley. It's a changing panoply of colors and plants.

◆ Put in the bones with hardy shrubs that will have a distinct blooming season, plus look good in winter.

◆ Have a succession of blooms for all three seasons.

◆ Keep paths and walks very simple.

◆ Use patio stones or flagstone near the house; pull up the grass and replace it with pea gravel or other such felicitous pathway material.

◆ Don't worry about adding a great deal of color as long as it all harmonizes. The Sugarmans stained the deck a sky-blue (with a hint of purple); the door trim is a deep green, and there's a red tinge to the cedar stripping. The garden evolves into green and purples as the season wears on. Somehow, it's all very restful.

Patios

Patios can be a misery. Usually, they are already installed and you have a problem. A condo with a patio has even more problems. You want to create a private retreat in this small space and not upset whatever your neighbors have set as standards. You can use plants to give a sense of privacy.

If you live in a condo, find out what the rules are, and work within their limits. It may be difficult, because you won't be able to change the common space and there may be just so much you can do with your own space. I've seen places in France where you could see an amazing array of gardens, even though they each have exactly the same configuration and must follow the same rules. What you see from above is the astonishing range of the human imagination. What you see from the road is a uniform wall of green, since almost all of them are hidden behind their own hedges. It's the individual perception of space that counts.

✦ If you are building a patio and garden from scratch, use an attractive local stone. This will be cheaper in the long run, because it won't be coming from a distance—so no import tax. It will also have a nice natural feel to it.

✦ Mark the edges with spray paint, lime or flour to get a feel for the scale of the patio in relation to the house.

✦ Get rid of weeds. Roundup, or glysophate, a systemic herbicide, unfortunately is beginning to show that it accumulates in the soil. This worries me, and I tend to use any available plastic held down by bricks or stone and let the sun do the work. This is called solarizing and is the safest way to kill weeds.

✦ Make sure the stone is sloped in such a way that it will drain easily.

✦ If this is to be a dry-laid patio, do the following: Add 6 inches of $3/4$-inch crushed stone, 1 to 2 inches of stone dust (ground-up rock). Once the flagstones are laid, sweep the stone dust over the patio to fill in spaces, then water. Repeat this technique several times until you feel it's firm. This will keep the stones from shifting.

✦ Choose a planting that will be comfortable for your neighbors, that will give you some cosseting and be easy on the eyes. Again, I'm suggesting soft gray/silver foliage mixed with stronger yellows and blues: If you have as least five hours of sun a day, plant caryopteris and Russian sage, *Perovskia,* both with silver foliage and blue blooms in the late summer or early autumn. They are wonderfully scented, almost like sage, and first-rate as screening. Work around them with plants such as leadwort, *Ceratostigma plumbaginoides.* It's a slow-to-spread groundcover that turns vermilion in autumn over brilliant blue flowers. There are lots of low-growing hardy geraniums that work well; lavenders, santolina, and curry plant all have dramatic silver foliage.

Pockets in Patios

You can enhance any patio by taking out a few bricks
or stones and adding a tiny pocket of plants. You will
have to make sure the scale fits the size of the patio. If
it's too small, it will look ditzy and meaningless. Too
large, and you'll wonder why you bothered putting in
an expensive patio.

You can see what Ted Johnston did in his patio (see
shots #9 and 9a). First, he measured how far away he
wanted to be from the borders surrounding the patio.
Then he made sure the pocket wasn't going to be in
the way of any established traffic pattern.

He lifted out the bricks in a suitable pattern, as well
as the ones easy to pull out. After removing most of
the soil, he backfilled with a mix of loam and compost
and planted up. He chose plants that love the warmth
of stones, such as lavender, sage and sedums.

6

Found Gardens: Pools, Parking Lots and Alleys

Can there be anything as unlovely as the ubiquitous abandoned space or parking lot? It might be at the front of your house or cluttering up a back alley. It might seem an unlikely place to garden, but installing a pocket garden can change the unpromising into a thing of beauty. You'll understand this better by studying Hy Rosenberg's garden (see shot #10). This was part of the alley outside a downtown law office. The existing space was not something Mr. Rosenberg wanted to look at, so when he decided to have large double windows installed, he asked landscape architect Dennis A. Winters to solve his problem.

THE ALLEY CONVERSION

Winters, whose company, Tales of the Earth, creates meditation gardens, has a design ethic that springs out of his own experience traveling and studying from Japan to Tibet, as well as from the needs of his clients. This garden shows the fruits of his experience.

The site was about the size of a car (6 feet wide and 17 feet long), a decrepit alcove filled with rubbish, discarded building materials, tar and gravel. Because the alley bespoke of nefarious nocturnal activity, the client wanted it shut out. The only entrance to the garden was to be from the office for security reasons as well as the above. Many lessons are to be learned from this project.

Winters is quick to point out that when you hire a designer, it is critical for the designer to listen to and *collaborate with* the client. In this case, the client, Hy Rosenberg, had a fascination with t'ai chi and yoga as well as a great love of hiking on the Bruce Trail and spending time exploring the city and its ravines. Winters felt some element of each of these interests should be expressed in the design.

He and his client also decided this should be a garden to move through rather than an object to contemplate. Simplicity was important in the solution to the problem—the composition should help overcome the confusion and turmoil outside the site. This sounds very much like a Japanese garden, but it's quintessentially a North American garden with some overtones of Oriental inspiration.

Apart from excluding aspects of the unlovely alley-way, they wanted to create a different world inside the space, but not at the expense of completely negating the outside world. Winters also wanted to celebrate the existence of fire escapes, the air-conditioning ducts going up the five- and six-story buildings all around. The height of the fence would be important in keeping cars out of sight but still allow the vitality of the alley to seep in.

There were a lot of other considerations as well: enclosure without being claustrophobic. The fence was based on the client's height, about 5 feet 9 inches. It ended up being 6 feet 3 inches high, which is the perfect height when standing inside the office. It's possible to look out beyond the fence and see the ambience of the buildings around, but the parked cars and parking-lot detritus are screened out. Here, Winters was dealing with mathematical proportions on one hand and sensitivity to what works on the other. It's now possible to move within the garden and not be distracted by the outside world.

To enlarge the sense of space within, Winters began by orienting the structure of the garden along a diagonal line. Next he broke up the space into two smaller units, developing a relationship between the two sides of the garden: positive and negative, dry and wet, male and female. On the male side, there are upward-thrusting sharper rocks, with a dry stream and a trellis that reaches skyward. On the female side, the garden is lower. This is where the water and the rounded stones are placed. And each side is modified to bring the female to the male and the male to the female. If one side is expressed as an extreme at the expense of the other, then all elements become discordant. As Winters points out: the pieces of the garden have to express an interactive whole.

He then layered the details in the garden. The eye moves from the fence down to something in front of it (a fountain, a Japanese maple, rocks), allowing the viewer to go through a whole series of experiences by the time the eye gets to ground level. You can see how effective a contemplative garden can be even in crowded city conditions.

Though you don't have to be religious or philosophical about creating a small garden space, having some underlying concept adds an element of profundity to the total garden experience.

The Construction

Winters dug out at least 18 inches of existing soil. There were, luckily, no toxic substances on the spot; but old buiding materials and trash had to come out. His search for the right stones to fulfill his vision took several months of scouring local stoneyards.

For instance, Winters wanted to capture the feel of Muskoka in the texture of the stones. The number of stones he chose wasn't as critical as it would be in an authentic Japanese garden. In Japan, each stone would have a name, a history, and evoke a certain poem. To get this kind of vitality, he cautions, the composition of stones *is* important. He likes to set them so they appear to talk to one another. His placement makes them come alive, and figures quite literally can appear. He always buries stones up to one-third underground for stability. Even bulky types of stone need this.

+ *The Soil:* The first application of triple mix proved to be a mistake, because it was much too porous and turned mushy. For building up the land he uses a screened pile run topsoil—a mixture of mostly sand and silt with hardly any clay or organic matter. It's more stable and doesn't settle as much as a soil higher in organic material. He uses this in really wet gardens to build up ground levels and then applies triple mix on top for planting
+ *The Water:* Water for the pond is stored in a lined pressure-treated wood tank $2^1/_2$ feet cubed. It's set underground and is covered with a pebble-covered cast iron grill. The circulating pump is inside the tank. Water coming out of the spout falls on one of the large rounded stones, then onto the small pebbles. In the same way the waves of Lake Ontario make the crackling sounds on the pebbles of the shore, the water of Hy's garden makes crackling sounds as it falls through the pebbles. It then drops into the ground and the tank as though falling into a limestone cave.
+ Though bamboo doesn't last in our climate, Winters points out, the client wanted it for the waterspout,

and it's had to be replaced several times. And the client is always right, since he's the one paying for it.

✦ *The Fence:* The fence has a 4-by-4 frame with 2-by-2s inside to give the rhythm of bamboo even though it doesn't actually resemble it. In this case, it was decided to achieve a feeling or a mood rather than make a direct copy. Here, the material is cedar with a clear stain, so it won't turn the natural silvery-gray.

✦ A contemplative garden is not to everyone's taste. Though the stones form the structure of the garden, plants are a part of the entire composition but not meant to stand out. They may be few, but they are choice. Here, the focal point is a Japanese maple, *Acer palmatum* 'Osakazuki.' The groundcovers, Irish moss, *Sagina subulata* 'Caespitosa'; Scotch moss, *Arenaria verna* 'Aurea'; sweet woodruff, *Galium odoratum*; and red epimedium, *Epimedium x rubrum*, make this a very easy garden to maintain.

TAKING BACK THE BASKETBALL COURT

Changing a site from tarmac to garden can take time, as I found out many years ago. We had a basketball hoop and the attendant asphalt to run around on for about 20 years before I decided to get rid of it all and make a pocket garden. Nature, as usual reclaiming its own, helped by turning the asphalt into a total mess over time. Trees and weeds were constantly banging their way through the surface. But pulling up the rest and getting rid of it was another problem. Each piece had to be hauled away through a narrow passage by hand—my son Chris's, I hasten to add.

Like many backyards in this city, the very end of the garden was used as a midden (a.k.a. garbage dump). We dug our way through almost a hundred years of ashes, glass and other bits and pieces from a former era. Bricks were cleaned and saved; old glass was cleaned and collected, as were the hundreds of marbles and children's toys (none very interesting).

Anything that was cement was used as a base to build up a small scree garden. The rest, unfortunately, headed to the landfill. Then restoring the soil to health became an absolute obsession. For three years, I threw all the leaves I could save from my own and neighbors' gardens on top of the soil. We kept a pile of soil on one side of the garden just to make a layer over the leaves to keep them from blowing about, though this usually wasn't a problem, since the area was fenced on three sides.

Each spring, my son would turn it over until it was rich with earthworms and ready to plant. By the time we felt it was ready, there wasn't a thing in sight. All the Manitoba maple saplings were pulled out, and after a month of solarizing, it was virtually weed-free.

Solarizing is a great technique for getting rid of weeds in a small, contained space:

+ Cover the area with black plastic or any kind of heavy cover that can be easily held down at the perimeter with bricks. Leave this in place for at least two to three weeks. Anything attempting to grow should be pretty much killed off by that time.

✦ If I were to do this again, I would add a layer of sand on top of the leaves to get a lighter, faster-draining soil in this heavy clay area.

The results of this work include a small border only 4 by 10 feet, which is chock-a-block with ornamental grasses, *Clematis integrifolia*, dwarf evergreens, a rose-bush and a *Tamarix ramosissima*, which is kept pruned to keep it in scale. Plus *Hosta* 'Ginko Craig,' *Salvia verticillata* 'Purple Rain' and a glorious golden oregano (see shot #11).

ALLEY GARDENING

I came across a hidden pocket garden one day when looking for a parking spot. Here, in an alley, was a small raised bed outside the garden gate jammed with plants against a background of vines crawling up the fence. It was utterly charming and known only to the parkers of cars.

It turned out to belong to the very person I was visiting, a gardener so modest she had never bothered to mention this part of her gardening life. She has an enchanting inner-city courtyard garden but is one of those people who can't bear to throw out anything. Ergo, what could be better than an alley garden. It was her present to the passerby, she says. New plants could be experimented with out there. In late spring, when she divides plants, the overflow goes into the alley. Rejected plants have space as well. She started with euonymus, then added several vines: honeysuckle, *Lonicera x brownii* 'Dropmore Scarlet'; Virginia creeper, *Parthenocissus quinquefolia*; climbing hydrangea, *Hydrangea petiolaris*; with silver lace vine, *Polygonum aubertii*, vaulting up a telephone pole. Thymes spill over the curb; extra chives, parsley, basil all find a home here, along with *Mentha aquatica*; sage, *Salvia officinalis*; and the masterstroke, an annual sprinkling of *Cosmos* 'White Sensation.'

Any ugly blank space, such as a lane between two houses, can be improved with containers jammed with plants. Look again at Jan Sugarman's formerly unattractive alleyway (see shot #1). She took the crazy paving rescued from the backyard reconstruction and piled it up in the alley in different heights. One plant found its way there, then another joined it. As each pot was added, she experimented with what would grow in this low light—only about five hours a day—that would also resist the assault of kids going through with bikes and toys and all the other usual traffic. She uses this space for new and exciting plants without having to worry about how they relate to anything but each other.

The pots are where she changes her color scheme from year to year. For instance, in one year, she concentrated on lime and maroon. She had

Plectranthus 'Ochre Flame,' and other forms in variegated limes, greens and grays. An ivy geranium called *Pelargonium* 'Crocodile' is an almost chlorotic lime green, deeply veined with maroon. Also included were golden variegated potato vine, *Solanum jasminoides,* a variegated lysimachia with yellow, cup-shaped flowers much like *Lysimachia nummularia* 'Aurea' but with foliage of lime-green and russet. Trailing tuberous begonias in orange and lime backed by a black sweet potato vine, *Ipomoea batatas* 'Blackie,' complete the theme. These are interesting and audacious ideas that might overwhelm a small garden, but the alley is an ideal area for experimentation.

In our own alley, I finally got it together when I had rickety old steps ripped out and new ones installed. The barbecue, which I insisted would never come on to the deck, has a new niche and is out of sight. On the steps, I put a large blue and white Chinese pot filled with ferns and a very white form of gardener's garters called *Phalaris arundinacea* 'Feesey's Form.' It's simple and looks elegant enough to make me want to keep the gate open so we can see it from the deck.

A POCKET DRIVEWAY GARDEN

The area next to a driveway is usually ignored. Get rid of anything mucky, but save rocks and slabs that you might want to keep for drainage. Pull out weeds, and solarize the soil to get rid of anything lurking about (see page 109). You can't have plants which will brush against the side of the car or which might suffer from having snow thrown on top of them.

✦ Some suggested plantings: a hedge of Japanese holly, *Ilex crenata* 'Compacta'; a littleleaf linden, *Tilia cordata,* underplanted with roses; foxgloves, *Digitalis*; cheddar pinks, *Dianthus*; and *Artemisia absinthium* 'Huntington.'

✦ A gorgeous selection of ornamental grasses along with dwarf evergreen plants such as rose daphne, *Daphne cneorum*; dwarf Alberta spruce, *Picea glauca* 'Albertiana Conica'; dwarf Hinoki false cypress, *Chamaecyparis obtusa* 'Nana'; dwarf mugo pine, *Pinus mugo* 'Compacta'; and one of my favorite plants, inkberry, *Ilex glabra,* which has wonderful, shiny black-green leaves all winter long.

SWIMMING POOL GARDENS

One of the most imaginative uses I've seen of a swimming pool was one completely filled in, with the sides built up for a terrace, the bottom a patio. A small pond was built into the sides.

When I first went into the garden, I was caught off-guard. I was sure something else had been here. And I was right. The swimming pool was in a shady spot and took up the whole of the yard, but no one wanted to use it. First, the concrete had to be cracked up to provide good drainage; then the gardener started filling in with clean rubbish he found from buildings being torn down. This was contoured to give him the terracing he needed in the space. He added a layer of gravel and a good triple mix and topped it with compost. Then he created a small pond on a shelf at the edge complete with a light, a small concrete statue and water plants.

If you have acquired an abandoned swimming pool beyond repair or have the good sense to prefer plants to paddling, try the following:

◆ Use construction felt to line the pool. This keeps soil in and lets water leach out the drain. Put in crushed stone, plus a layer of gravel to make it even. Then add the soil.
◆ To have a pond within the pool, fill most of the pool space with a base of gravel and then topsoil in which to plant. Set a preform in place. Add flat rocks around the edges to give it a strong natural shape.

And if you've inherited an above-ground pool, try what one adventurous gardener did. The pool collapsed and left a gaping, ugly scar. He hauled away the debris slowly and painfully and was left with a 20-foot-diameter hole. This was slowly filled in layer by layer with sand, compost and clean fill. A semi-circular garden slowly emerged with steps leading down to it.

TIPS

In recovering lost spaces, use some of the following:

✦ When doing any kind of construction, lift off all the good soil and keep it to one side. Return it to the site when you've finished work.

✦ Stockpile debris, then cover with compost and sand and start a small raised bed or scree area.

✦ If you have a fireplace, dump ashes right on top of the snow—they'll percolate downward. Don't use the ash from chemical logs, however.

✦ Add pots of brightly colored plants to low-traffic areas that need some sprucing up.

7

Gardening on High: Balconies, Roofs and Window Boxes

Balconies pose no more problems to the pocket gardener than any other constricted space. Most balconies, regardless of size, can be transformed completely with a little imagination and a lot of the right containers. But you must know what limits there are to your balcony garden.

Begin by checking out what the building's rules are. Find out whether there are structural restrictions, such as how much weight is allowed; what watering specifications there are (you don't want to be dripping on the neighbors below); whether you're allowed to paint or not; and whether plants hanging over the railing or balustrade will contravene some code.

The most significant thing about a balcony is that

you look at it from wherever you sit in the living room. This is where your design starts. Spend time on a comfy sofa, do some creative staring, and take stock of what's already there. Your view is framed by windows, curtains and the balcony itself. Use your imagination to think about how to meld the outside with the inside and have a green barrier against the rest of the world. A balcony garden is no less a sanctuary than is any other.

Balconies are usually too small to be grandiose, but that doesn't mean to say they can't be clever and stylish. Think of it as a part of the living room, and consider how you'll make the two work together. By choosing a color or style extant in the living room and moving it outside, you can achieve a fair amount of unity.

One thing I like to do in the summer, for instance, is to give my whole place a much airier look by moving furniture and decorative elements outside. This gives a sense of continuity between the two spaces as well and makes the house feel like it's extended right into the garden. This principle is even more important in an apartment.

Consider the flooring first. It may be possible to use the same colors or similar carpeting outside, such as sisal, carpet ends or even old Oriental rugs. Any one of these could give the feel of an outdoor room to the tiniest of balconies. Orientals, for instance, were intended for abusive treatment and can be bought secondhand inexpensively, considering the amount of wear you'll get out of them. One of the balconies we photographed had a lovely Oriental rug, which has taken the brunt of the weather for years and was old when it was purchased. It looks warm and just about the same as it did ten years ago.

Painted carpets are becoming popular and provide what could be a brilliant solution. These canvas-backed paintings can be done cheaply, and you can go wild with a design that will make the floor of your balcony enchanting, or at least make it just disappear. You need to have "sized" canvas before you start the design, and there are books that will show exactly how to go about making one.

These days, painted concrete has taken on a whole new dimension with new concrete-wash products. They are water-based and it doesn't matter how much damage has been done to the existing concrete. No base is required. If you want a design, it's easy enough to rent a special machine that will bite into the concrete and create a repetitive pattern or make it look like blocks of stone. Be sure the concrete is relatively clean. Then apply the wash with a circular motion (no straight lines, which will make it look dull); this will create a mottled effect. Let dry, then add another new color if you want a denser effect. The age and chemical properties of the concrete will make the final look. When you are happy with the result, apply a seal. (Concrete Colorwash Systems is just one of the companies that makes this product.)

If an awning isn't provided, the next move should be to install one. This will give you privacy and, if you're facing south or west, some protection from blazing afternoon sun. It also gives a sense of being cosseted and continues the feeling that this is an extension of the living room. It's another method of framing the view as well. A good awning will throw interesting light; others will add a decorative touch. An awning will definitely add to the amount of time you'll be able to spend on the balcony, since you'll be able to sit outside or eat there when it's raining.

Consider installing a mirror at one or both ends of the balcony. This will reflect the plantings back to you and provide an illusion of space. I like mirrors everywhere in my garden. And a balcony has no problems with children bunging a baseball into it. If you have it at one end of the balcony, fix it in place so that there is a slight tilting back into the living room. This will extend your view.

✦ If there is decorative ironwork edging, make sure that the containers echo this formality. Don't hang the boxes on the top; set them on the floor so that the plants can climb up and spill over the ground and downward. It will make for a much more gardeny feeling.

✦ Even the smallest balcony can afford to give up a small bit of wall space for a miniature water feature. You'll find extremely small, self-circulating pumps that can move the water from one container to another. These can be fixed to a wall with concrete brackets and the pipe fixed behind so that it won't be seen.

ROOFTOP GARDEN

First, check what the roofing surface is. You could have asphalt or chipped tiles. It could be in dreadful condition. You must make sure that you are gardening on a leak-proof surface and that you don't puncture the roof once you start construction. Check out how water and snow drain off the roof by dousing it with water and seeing where puddles accumulate. One of the boons to modern rooftop gardening is the invention of really handsome wooden decks built in sections. Easy to transport, they can be used to make a walkway through raised planters or assembled to make a small deck, which is a good way to spread out the weight.

✦ All the caveats apply about weight, but you also have to figure out how to bring soil and equipment through the house without making a huge mess. In an apartment building, you have to find out how much weight elevators will hold.

✦ Again, work on the microclimate you're stuck with, including how much sun (afternoon sun can be a killer for plants) and exposure.

✦ Plan a space for storage. A pillow-covered bench with hinged top will hold an amazing amount of stuff. At least you won't need to accommodate a lawn mower.

✦ Make some kind of shelter from the midday sun: There are new lightweight tents open on four sides that are easy to install and look airy and bright. If you use one of the huge market umbrellas, make sure it's anchored solidly and be prepared for bird droppings.

✦ Lightweight, soilless soil is good because it holds water more efficiently.

✦ It's important to check for dryness regularly.

✦ Line clay pots with waterproof plastic (though you must punch a drainage hole), add water-retaining granules to the soil, and use a gravel mulch to keep the amount of watering down.

The Wind

It won't be news that the problem most balconies and roofs share is the dreaded wind factor. It's astonishing how devastating the wind can be, and it increases the higher up you live. If the wind is an important factor, start making a sturdy wind-resistant screen before you attempt anything else. Trellis or bamboo shades well-anchored in place are two good solutions. I like to use square lattice for almost anything from disguising a crummy-looking wall to masking the compost.

✦ Make trellis with 4-inch openings to provide a good see-through appearance. When clad with vines, it will be a proper windbreak.

+ Cedars will do well in large enough boxes, but it's important to make sure that they are well-anchored and won't blow over and that the space can take the amount of weight.

+ Consider how you'll make a barrier between yourself and the next-door neighbor. Climbers are a natural to get in immediately. You *can* have perennial vines if you have large enough containers, and that's a good place to start. Most balconies can accept containers about 15 inches deep and 14 to 15 inches wide, which is about the right size for the root system to survive. Again, you'll have to check the weight and see whether it's acceptable to your building's management. Then get containers built, or buy them as large as you possibly can afford.

+ Slow-growing but really satisfying vines such as ivies would be my first choice. They stay evergreen, so there is winter interest as well, which should be a consideration. You can have clematis, Virginia creeper, even wisteria, although the last two are rampant and they could mean a lot of work keeping them cut to size.

+ Window boxes and containers should be kept away from the edges for safety's sake, which means looking for plants that are low-growing so that they won't block too much light.

+ If the wind velocity is high, you won't be able to grow evergreens or thin-stemmed flowers such as lilies.

Watering

This is always going to be a problem. If you don't have an outdoor tap or can't install one easily and cheaply, then consider getting a small hose system that can be hooked up to the most readily available tap. This will save a lot of trucking back and forth carrying big cans of water. In hot weather, you'll be doing this twice a day.

✦ Add polymers to the soil mix to hold in water. The soil should still feel moist when you stick a finger in up to the first knuckle.

✦ If you have the space, rig up a hose to the kitchen tap and make it long enough to reach the balcony. Keep it rolled up under the sink when it's not in use.

✦ If this is totally impractical, face the fact that you'll have at least half an hour of watering by hand every day. Fill cans and jugs the night before so that chemicals will have time to evaporate. This is a good rule for all containers.

✦ There are some pretty good wick watering systems and kits you might want to consider if you're off on holidays. They consist of a central water source, with wicks leading off to the various containers that will suck up the water when needed. You can do this yourself by setting a big pail on a slight riser and having wicks running out to each of the pots.

✦ When on holidays, make sure to lower the awning. This will help to protect the plants.

THE WELL-DESIGNED BALCONY

We chose two balconies that embodied elegance in furnishings and choice of plants but were also the size of most normal balconies. Peter Jackman and Mark McLaine (see shots #12 and 13) are lucky enough to have two balconies, which are only 7$^1/_2$ feet wide and yet give a feeling of opulence. They have solved a great many of their visual problems by keeping to a unified theme in color and style, indoors and out. They painted the boxes, latticework and even the decking a greenish-black. This blends in anonymously with the building, since the rules were that nothing could stand out. They chose blue as an accent in plants and on the striped padding of chairs and awning, which gives a sprightly air to both balconies. The fabric used is called Sunbrella, which sheds pollution and won't fade in the sun.

+ Over the decking in one area, they used small Oriental rugs, again an echo of the living room and bedrooms that open onto a balcony.
+ Lighting is important on these charming balconies. They have Greek-key light fixtures. Keeping the voltage low is important both for building codes and maintaining the formal appearance.
+ To hide all the paraphernalia connected with both barbecuing and gardening, they bought two large windows and frames. The trim is in blue, and the glass has been painted out with weatherproof black paint. It's a great background to a seating area close

by, and they can stack up equipment next to the barbecue.

✦ They have a water feature set into one of the raised beds that fits in with the unified whole. The preformed plastic liner has a small bubbling fountain. That and a small statue of an angel seated on one edge give it a formal feeling. It also cuts the sound of the busy street below. Again, water is very heavy, and weights would have to be checked out.

The Plants

✦ The raised boxes on the Jackman/McLaine balcony are large enough to accommodate perennial vines such as Virginia creeper. The boxes are lined with Styrofoam and drilled with drainage holes.

✦ They have found that if pots are large enough, it's completely unnecessary to store them for the winter. They cover them with plastic to keep them from getting wet, which will expand the soil and crack the pot. In spring, they replace the top 2 inches of soil and add mulch.

✦ They use a base planting of perennials, grasses and vines, then add favorite annuals. They successfully grow other vines, such as silver lace, bittersweet and clematis, on their ninth-floor balcony without worrying too much about the wind factor.

✦ Must-have annuals are geraniums, *Pelargonium*, morning glories; sweet peas; and marguerite daisies.

Gloria Bishop's balcony (seen on our cover and in shot #14) is 25 feet long by 6 feet wide, and it gives her enough work to be able to spend a good half-hour a day on watering and deadheading. It makes her feel that she's just as much a gardener now as when she had one on the ground. In one corner, there is an old sewing-machine base with a large round top that can be quickly set up in spring and stored easily in winter.

For the floor, she chose a soft Mediterranean shade of terra-cotta, and for the inside of the metal railing, a tawny oak color inspired by the stand of oak trees that surrounds the building. The two hues continue the same palette of the apartment.

At one end of the balcony, she has a seating area with a small table. When she entertains, she places a larger plywood top on it and has room to fit in three with comfort. The top is stored unobtrusively the rest of the time. She also uses an Oriental rug in this area. A pink fabric-covered banquette built across one end serves to store empty pots. Tools are stored in an apple basket, and spare soil (things always need a bit of topping up, she says) is kept in a plastic-lined wicker laundry hamper, which is also used as a side table.

✦ She fills the pots on the sewing table with chives, sorrel, two kinds of parsley, oregano, mint and a variety of lettuces.

✦ She chooses a mix of purple, coral, reds and yellows in the same range of tints as in the decor of the apartment. The window boxes are filled with trailing lobelias, lipstick plants and impatiens that bush out over the season. Tuberous begonias come in all the colors she favors.

✦ See page 168 to read how she set up her little fountain.

✦ For winter storage, Bishop uses what she calls the foster-care plan. She grows hostas, ferns and lilies and puts them in a friend's garden for the winter.

PLANTING SUGGESTIONS AND BALCONY CARE

✦ Before putting out any plants, give them a good shower. In this microclimate, any aphids or other pests lurking about will have a chance to thrive.

✦ Be sure to start watering all raised boxes and large, weatherproof containers as soon as the soil warms up in early spring. You'll find you probably are ahead of those gardening on the ground.

✦ Try a theme such as an all-white garden if you spend only your evenings on the roof or balcony. Nicotiana would be my first choice, one of the highly scented ones; and moonflower, *Ipomoea*, would be a must. Then add white impatiens, petunias, lilies (if you have a wind-protected spot) and any of the silver-foliaged lamiums or pulmonarias.

9 & 9a

Here are two shots of Ted Johnston's patio with pockets taken out of it. They have become such a feature that they are the first thing most people comment on when they come into the garden. He used sun- and warmth-loving plants such as lavender, sage and a variety of sedums. See page 101.

10

Hy Rosenberg's garden designed by Dennis Winters has all the magic of a Japanese garden but is firmly rooted in North America. See page 103 for a complete description.

SPRING

✦ Plant all the little bulbs in profusion. Work out a color scheme, and fill pots with them after having put them in the fridge for six weeks. I'd put in narcissus such as 'Tête à Tête,' 'Pipit' and 'February Gold' or a pure white, scented one such as 'Thalia.' Violas, crocuses, muscari and scilla all make very good container plants.

✦ Rosemary, lavender and other herbs should be planted as early as possible.

✦ Hostas will survive very nicely in well-protected large pots if they aren't subject to freeze-thaw conditions. But I like them enough in pots to consider putting in new ones each year and giving them away for safekeeping to friends in the fall.

SUMMER

✦ Keep all plants deadheaded. In such a small space, you want everything to look as perfect as possible. Deadheading is simple: Just clip off anything that looks past its prime. This will also encourage plants to keep on blooming, since it's part of the genetic code to make seed (something you don't want in a pocket garden).

✦ Snapdragons, gloriosa daisies, carnations, stocks and cosmos are all good summer-blooming plants.

✦ Vegetables: Cherry tomatoes such as 'Sweet 100,' 'Sweet Million' and 'Tiny Tim' are space savers that will produce lovely fruit.

✦ Keep vines twining around their props, and dead-head them regularly. This is especially good for clematis. I've found that some forms will even try to bloom again.

✦ Give everything a hit of nutrition every couple of weeks. A fish fertilizer about half the strength recommended in the instructions is good. If you make compost, this should be added regularly. Soil in containers becomes depleted fairly rapidly. Compost or manure tea is easy to make: Fill a container with water and let a bag of either compost or manure sit inside for a week or so. Cut it in half with water when you add it to the plants.

AUTUMN

✦ Cut off yellowing hosta leaves as soon as you see them. But keep on deadheading annuals such as impatiens, which will carry on right up until frost. And if you get them in time, you'll be able to move them indoors where they may survive the winter.

✦ Remove annual vines before they look too sad. Plant bulbs in the largest containers and give them a good watering.

WINTER

✦ It will be obvious on your very first winter that you need something evergreen. Ivies are a great investment. But you must go into winter having done a thorough watering job on all the permanent plantings. Evergreens will continue to transpire throughout the season and will become desiccated in high winds. Make sure they get watered very deeply, and apply an antidesiccant spray.

✦ Perennials such as candytuft, *Iberis sempervirens*, will now come into their own again, as will evergreen European ginger, *Asarum europaeum*, the large-leaved *Bergenia cordifolia* and any tough ornamental grass, such as blue oat grass, *Helictotrichon sempervirens*.

WINDOW BOXES

A window box can be very satisfying for the pocket gardener. You can have boxes in any size or the shape of any window. It's an almost ideal way to frame your view of the world and offers an inordinate amount of pleasure. Even those without a garden can have a window box no matter how small. The benefits of this garden-in-miniature have been confirmed by studies done in such places as seniors' lodges. As soon as an individual has responsibility for a plant, even if it's only one, the sense of future and of self-worth shoots upward. So if you have someone in your life who says he or she doesn't have a green thumb or hates plants, consider this advice: Anyone who gardens feels better about themselves and the world.

First, take into account what you have to put a window box on. Make sure there's a ledge wide enough so that there's no chance the box will tip over, because the natural habit of most plants is to grow outward toward the sun. Build a shelf where you can install large L-brackets to give it as much support as possible. Place the box so that soil, rotting foliage and other organic matter won't affect the ledges or sill it sits on. To be twice as safe, set the box on a few bricks so that it doesn't actually touch the frame of the house.

Drainage is another matter. If you have to prop up the window box, consider how and when you'll be doing your watering. If you have a window box over a pedestrian walkway, you should be considerate enough to water when there's nobody around.

Window boxes have one tricky thing in their design: They must look good from inside as well as outside. So remember that when you are working with the plants. And keep in mind that they should also have charm in winter as well as summer.

We are used to thinking about annuals for window boxes, but that is essentially limiting. If you approach a window box in much the same way as you do any garden, you'll start with thinking about the basic structure, or the "bones," of your design. Have a color scheme that will go with what you have not only inside the house but also outside. No point in having a flaming orange up against a red brick wall. One will cancel out the other. Dark walls scream for pale colors; and a white wall wants to have dark, rich tones.

Spring Window-Box Plants

I love grape hyacinths, *Muscari*, as edging plants, and window boxes are no exception for showing off their cobalt-blue loveliness. Bulbs do extremely well in window boxes: scillas, chionodoxa and the smallest of species tulips and narcissus. Then I like to have a combination of pansies, which now have such velvety, gorgeous colors, you can do endless things with them. From black to purple, to all the colors of expensive lingerie, there's a pansy. They will do well no matter how you abuse them. I know, I've been there and done that. I also like to add perennials such as *Artemisia pontica* or *A. ludoviciana* 'Silver King' or 'Valerie Finnis,' all of which might be invasive in other parts of the garden but do okay here in the most adverse conditions. Then I will add something highly contrasty, such as *Lobelia* 'Crystal Palace,' a brilliant cobalt-blue that shines even in the shade. Other invasive plants, such as snow-in-summer, *Cerastium tomentosum*, can look good in and out of bloom in a window box.

Summer Window-Box Plants

+ Before you switch into summer gear, be sure to lift all bulbs and trim out any other fading spring plants. Add new soil and compost, and soak well enough for water to run out the bottom before you start a new planting.
+ The age-old favorites always look charming—petunias, lobelias and geraniums, *Pelargonium*—but you limit yourself mightily. You might want one or all of these plants, but go further in your design.
+ Herbs are superb window-box plants: rosemary, thyme, tarragon, mint (there are now dozens of kinds from variegated to pineapple), parsley and, of course, basil if you have the right sun conditions (at least four hours a day).

Winter Window-Box Plants

There's no point in having a window box empty in winter. Artemisias can form a background, almost nothing kills them, and they can be used in winter to prop up the colored twigs cut from red-stemmed dogwood. As I've mentioned before, *A. pontica*, an otherwise vicious spreader, behaves itself in a window box. You can also use:

+ Almost any ivy. 'Baltica' is the hardiest and won't get rampant. Variegated forms such as 'Little Diamond' and 'Sulphur Heart' add a bit of sophistication.

✦ Dwarf (almost bonsai-sized) evergreens such as junipers and false cypresses, *Chamaecyparis*. All will make a good show.

✦ A collection of pinecones, the larger the better, if you don't have squirrels vandalizing your boxes.

✦ Cedar lengths looped around boxes filled with dried grasses, ornamental kale and other dried, seed-bearing stems.

✦ And don't forget that old standby—the bright red twigs of dogwood, *Cornus*. Cover them with bows and lights, and you've got Christmas.

Make a Window Box

✦ Buy three lengths of cedar or pine, $7^1/_2$ by $20^1/_2$ inches; three short pieces, $7^1/_2$ by $11^1/_2$ inches; and end caps, $7^1/_2$ by 9 inches.

✦ For a larger box: three $7^1/_2$ by $27^1/_2$ inches; three $7^1/_2$ by $18^1/_2$ inches; and end caps $7^1/_2$ by 9 inches.

✦ Add molding 1 to 2 inches wide to give a finishing touch.

✦ Glue and nail the pieces together.

✦ Paint inside and out to seal the surface.

8

Retrieved Spaces: Sidewalks, Raised Beds and Berms

Gardeners by nature are greedy creatures. We who have a little space want more. I certainly do. A few years ago, to alleviate my frustration about having such a small front garden, I decided to put in an extension—a pocket garden. With son wielding a sledge-hammer in tow, I guided the hacking out of seven squares of sidewalk—our side of a mutual walk between our house and the one south of us. As you can see by the photograph of my sidewalk garden (see shot #15), it's next to a raised bed and seems to nestle up against it quite happily. The space we took up is about 12 feet long and 18 inches wide; it doesn't seem like much, but it holds a lot of plants.

Some day, we'll have a lovely path alongside this

little pocket garden, but for the moment, my neighbor's side is still the same old disintegrating concrete. The garden itself, however, is so successful that neighbors stop constantly to look at its progress. The garbage persons have even stopped throwing cans and lids into it—a garden triumph on this street.

After painfully removing the concrete, we discovered an incredible amount of detritus that had gone into filling the hole before the bed was made for the concrete. It took a huge effort to dig it out completely and get rid of the mess—buried junk, sand, gravel and masses of roots. I did keep some of the gravel to use for drainage. We were looking at pretty dead soil after all those decades of concrete covering. But the nearby raised bed had been crawling with worms, so I figured they'd find their way into something new and delicious.

We were also dealing with the feeder roots of the nearby silver maple. This is a major city tree, and not necessarily the right one. But some 80 years ago, our politicians decided that this species is the one that would line our streets. All the trees are now in the process of dying from old age, pollution and abuse.

I felt bad at what we were doing to our old tree, but not enough to hold me back from digging down a good 18 inches. We backfilled with a layer of washed gravel, then filled with a rich mix of topsoil, manure and compost. I watered, then top-dressed the whole area with more compost and waited a couple of weeks for the soil to settle. I had to cover it with plastic netting to keep every dog and cat on the street from using it as a litter box.

Then came the decision of what to put in. Starting *tabula rasa* with an area like this is one of my favorite moments in gardening. For an artist, it would be like starting with a blank canvas or a blank sheet of paper. It's all potential.

The garbagemen (and they *were* all men) could not cope with this; they threw lids, bags and anything else they felt like on top of the baby plants. No amount of heated discussion could dissuade them from this bad habit. So I decided that the area closest to the street should have a tallish shrub and some unkillable artemisias to try to keep a dividing line between that edge and the part closer to the house. Once they were installed, the woody plants helped buttress the smaller, more fragile plants against the weekly assault.

I found an old *Spiraea bumalda* 'Waterii' that I'd always hated in its location and put it in this difficult spot. In spite of being yanked out of a very old resting place and being exposed to the street, that constant miracle of nature occurred—it thrived. *Artemisia ludoviciana* 'Silver King' is the hardiest of the hardy plants (a little too hardy in some parts of the garden because it will spread like crazy). It did well here, too. Some wild asters found their way from different parts of the neighborhood, and I didn't discourage them until the glorious ornamental grass was mature enough. Northern sea oats, *Chasmanthium latifolium*, is my favorite grass, and it was placed in a prominent position next to a variegated iris.

The rest of the area proved a good place to put lots of low-growing plants with an informal edging of lavenders. There is just enough light in this spot to allow these great plants to grow. It was also a bit of serendipity. The lavenders at the edge of the raised bed had seeded themselves along the edge. Anything that will seed itself in such a position must be meant to stay.

Groundcovers such as lamiums proved to be too large for the area but the smaller form of thrift, *Armeria maritima*, suits it very well. Exquisite small plants such as a variegated arabis, golden campanula and a tiny groundcovering rose all made their way here. It led to the decision to keep the plants small with lots of variety.

To make this kind of a pocket garden, you will have to have a cooperative neighbor. Any sidewalk can be treated this way:

✦ If it's a dark alley sidewalk, take half of it, keeping in mind that you may still have to use part of the space for walking. One good solution I've seen was what became the work area of a garden. The area is at the side of the house, out of sight from everything else. The cement was removed altogether, and the soil improved much the same way as I did in my own garden. Two-foot-square patio stones were placed at random so that a casual walk appeared. Everything else was graveled, and plants were introduced to create an almost tapestrylike pattern. A large pot guarded the entrance and gave the area definition.

✦ If you can't break up the concrete of a sidewalk, you can drill holes so there will be some drainage and build raised beds.

Vines

Cover up any unsightly walls, even sightly ones. It will give the feeling of well-being as you pass through the area. And if the area is very shady, you can start with the following vines: Japanese hydrangea vine, *Schizophragma hydrangeoides*; climbing hydrangea, *Hydrangea petiolaris*; Virginia creeper, *Parthenocissus quinquefolia*; five-leaf akebia, *Akebia quinata*; scarlet firethorn, *Pyracantha coccinea*, which can also be espaliered along wire.

✦ If you are going to grow any of these vines up a wall, you've got to make sure the soil preparation is first-rate. Then give thought to the kind of support you'll be using.

✦ Lattice is always good. It can be attached straight into brick or concrete, but make sure there is a 1-inch space between wall and trellis or any other kind of support system. This will give a modicum of air circulation.

◆ In Europe, they use huge eyehooks with wire stretched between to let bougainvillea grow along. This is a good method for espaliering.

RAISED BEDS

Normally, you wouldn't think of a raised bed as a pocket garden, but that's an attitude that should be changed. Raised beds are incredibly useful. Planting above ground level (which is what a raised bed is) can avoid floods and frost. They are an ideal solution for anyone who is gardening on shallow soil (at the cottage, for instance). And they can be a boon to the handicapped or to those who've developed arthritis in the knees or have difficulty bending. For that matter, they can be important to any pocket of space.

Drainage is one of the essentials to all good gardening, and the raised bed can solve drainage problems in one fell swoop. Lousy drainage can make life hell for roots and cause all sorts of suffering through disease and stress. The raised bed is also just about the only way to go for those who live in frigid areas or on top of solid clay.

Raised beds mean that the soil warms up more rapidly in spring, and since it consists of the best-quality loam and lots of compost as topdressing, you find things grown in raised beds will flourish.

I've tried two ways of raising beds: digging down to create lowered paths and then adding soil to the adjacent borders; or piling on soil and organic matter behind a face of rocks or wood. Whichever method you use, think in terms of working from 12 to 18 inches in height.

Another effective way of using a raised bed is to get rid of an old stump. You can build a bed around the stump with either rocks or wood and fill it with soil and compost. Eventually, the stump will rot down and the bed will settle. Make sure that you can take off the top layer of rocks or wood, and place plants so that they will spill over and soften the edges.

If you want to plant vegetables, make sure the site will receive at least six hours of sun a day. Don't design anything that you can't reach easily from either side. The optimum length for simple construction is about 10 feet; the width is up to your arm's reach.

A word of warning about construction materials: Pressure-treated lumber will leach out far more arsenic and other toxic substances than is allowed by law. Don't put this around a vegetable patch or anywhere near where children play. I wouldn't use it near any living plant unless it was lined with heavy plastic that's been pierced for drainage. It's been suggested that if you use pressure-treated wood, allow it to weather for several months. In my experience, you can never allow enough time.

Raised beds can be any shape, but obviously a wooden one will give beds a geometric pattern. If you use stone, you can be more organic about the form.

+ Cedar and other weatherproof wood is expensive but will last a very long time. I have raised beds that have been in place for 18 years because we used good wood lined with plastic then stained.
+ Backfill with a good mix of soil, compost and cocofiber or peat moss to hold moisture in the soil. I use half loam, plus a quarter and a quarter. If I happen to have lots of it around, I add more compost and would top-dress with compost anyway. This is true especially if it's a small bed.

I remade one bed that had been devastated each year by the flood. Few things survived the assault of freeze-thaw which hit that part of the garden. I changed all that a few years ago by making this area into a raised bed about 18 inches high: I took out the remaining plants, piled up a soil-compost mixture with a small amount of cocofiber added, then lined the edges with stones to hold back the soil. I planted so intensely that this was made almost unnecessary. Because we are on a base of clay, I also added horticultural sand to the top like a mulch. Over time, it will keep the soil light and friable.

Absolutely everything thrives. I made this a blue and yellow foliage section. Small golden hostas gleam next to the gray-green foliage of such plants as *Corydalis flexuosa* 'Blue Panda' and *Aquilegia flabellata* 'Nana Alba.' There is a golden filipendula, a selection of silvery-leaved pulmonarias and a strange-looking

11

Author Marjorie Harris' reclaimed basketball court. See page 110.

12 & 13

Peter Jackman and Mark McLaine's two balconies have differing moods and light conditions. See page 125 for an explanation of these comfortable, well-designed balconies.

plant with carmine-splotched leaves called *Tovara virginiana*. The background planting in this shady area is Solomon's seal, *Polygonatum multiflorum*, which has arching stems with green-tipped white flowers not unlike bleeding hearts along the stem. I love this plant, but watch it—once established, it will travel by thick, hard-to-remove rhizomes.

THE BERM

I have liked the idea of berms since the first one was installed in my garden in 1986. A berm is considered any raised, rounded form usually more than 3 feet high. Our berm was created because of necessity: what to do with all the sod that had been lifted to make way for a complete garden. Flip over the sod and make a berm was the neat answer. The placement was important, because the berm, 24 feet long and 7 feet wide, was going to be installed only once.

What's really great about this berm is that my neighbor has now installed one the same size to mirror my own, and it makes both our gardens seem twice as big.

Berms create their own microclimate. A north side can be a mini frost hollow; a south-facing one can be a sun-baked oasis. Berms have many functions, not the least is being an ideal way to screen out neighbors, a nasty road or a railroad track. It's far more effective in cutting noise than a windbreak of trees.

You can make a berm any size, but it should be

strictly in scale with the garden you are dealing with. Plantings topping the berm will give you the much-needed barrier.

If you are particularly ambitious, you'll have to get a professional to grade the berm. In a pocket garden, however, a good spade and lots of sweat will more than likely do the trick.

It's important to install plants as quickly as possible, because this rise is vulnerable to erosion. I wanted to go at it slowly because I was just starting out and covered it with creeping Jenny, *Lysimachia nummularia.* This little plant leaps along, has a flush of yellow flowers in spring and usually has to be pulled out aggressively in a couple of years. It has a mind of its own, so don't use it unless you are prepared to do the work of hauling it out once it has done its job. Other plants such as hostas, ferns and pulmonarias did a much better, albeit slower, job.

The berm also has the beauty of height. Now this was much needed in this section of the garden. Semi-evergreen viburnums; mountain laurel, *Kalmia*; *Pieris japonica* 'Mountain Fire'; a very special little magnolia; and a species of rhododendron are giving it a dramatic effect on the topmost part of the contour.

Another consideration about berming is that it will give some shape to an otherwise dull, flat lot. Don't pimple up a space with a whole lot of little rises with one tree stuck on top. This form of landscaping is seen around here far too often, usually in front of grand houses, and it looks ridiculous. The other caveat is don't overberm. A berm that's too large will overwhelm a small space. Once again, scale is everything.

9

Scree, Gravel, Cracks and Crevices

To start with, let's get this term, scree, straight. Imagine a rocky mountain crevice, or think of the tailings left behind by the last Ice Age: broken stone in a multitude of sizes. Great drainage material. In nature, a scree is usually piled up against a cliff or mountainside.

The mountainous location, the stone, and swiftly moving water make screes incredibly successful at drainage, and the plants that live on them have evolved to survive on available rain (quite often from a local glacier). You may not have mountains or a glacier, but you can take that very same composition and put it to service in your own pocket garden. The job here is to replicate this situation but also to make it look aesthetic.

Scree gardens can be the ideal solution to very difficult circumstances. Rocky ground, sandy soil, little or no soil at all will lend itself to a scree garden. Many are, by nature, small places found in crevices, something which suits us here. The good thing about scree is that fussy plants of consuming interest can be used in the site, plants such as lewisias, drabas and androsaces that you don't want lost in the lushness of other perennials.

The most natural-looking scree bed would, of course, be between two splendid rocks tumbling down a small rise. But it doesn't matter—any raised bed can be turned into scree. A note of caution here: You'll need 2 to 3 feet of depth for the plants to do their best. If the plants' root systems are deep, their chances of survival will be that much greater.

In creating a scree, the first and most important principle is superb drainage. Alpines like lots of water, but only *en passant*. If you are gardening on clay, get ready to dig down and then add plenty of fill. It's one way to get rid of a lot of old bits and pieces that have been hanging about.

I made a specialized berm to accommodate all the junk that I thought was nontoxic taken up from areas we were pulling apart. There were concrete pilings from a deck that would have cost a fortune to take to the landfill. Then other chunks of stone were part of the general debris scattered about, broken bits of pots and cinders, since part of the backyard was a dumping ground for furnace ashes.

These were placed carefully in a semicircle to give some shape to the pocket. Then we added a layer of washed gravel and a few bags of horticultural sand to fill in the holes. If I did this again, I'd have a much thicker layer of sand just to bump up the drainage to make it very sharp. A small amount of soil and compost were added to top it off, then stepping-stones placed so that I could put my foot into the bed without disturbing plants. The height was about 2 feet; width 9 feet; and depth $4^1/4$ feet. It was an early-morning bed with about five hours of sun. One serious mistake in all this work: I put it far too close to a birch tree. I had to contend with dusting leaf drop off the bed by hand. I'd put it in a more isolated site next time.

Scree and rock gardeners are absolutely fanatic about the mix used for plants. I'm quoting two of the gurus of rock gardening, both of whom have written fascinating books on the subject.

Lincoln Foster's mix: 1 part loam; 2 parts coarse leaf mold or peat, sheep manure and bonemeal. Turn thoroughly with $1/8$- to $3/4$-inch gravel. The final blend should be 1 part loam-humus to 4 parts rock. He suggests laying a 2-inch layer of leaves over the drainage material before filling the excavation with soil mix. Top-dress with manure and bonemeal plus leaf mold in early spring and late fall. (From *Rock Gardening* by Lincoln Foster.)

Will Ingerwersen's mix: 2 parts loam or good top spit (level) garden soil, 1 part fine-grade moss peat or leaf mold, and 1 part sharp sand or fine grit. Assemble ingredients, add a sprinkling of bonemeal. Use no other fertilizer. (From *Alpines in Colour* by Will Ingerwersen.)

Landscape designer David Tomlinson recommends using Granular A—the gravel used for roadside verges. If anything more is needed, he adds a bit of leaf mold and some sandy soil. This is recommended for high alpine plants. For meadow plants, such as pasque flowers, *Pulsatilla*, he would have a mix of one-third sandy soil to two-thirds Granular A.

Alpines are plants that come from mountain areas or from areas that have similar conditions. They can grow up to 2 feet but are usually small given their original windblown sites. Our general assumption is that it is a small plant that emanates from a rosette or bun (little hummocky-shaped things). This means you can grow lots of them in a confined space. If you need one generalization, they are usually from temperate regions.

Ingerwersen writes that one important point about a temperate climate "is its ability to support exotic plants from other climes. In fact, in such a climate, plants can be grown from both the Tropics and the Arctic regions of the world." And, he points out, 50 percent of plants grown in rock gardens have never seen a mountain.

We're lucky that most of the alpines we do find in nurseries are raised in the garden and not taken from the wild. We have them because a few intrepid souls have taken seeds from sites all over the world and brought them into nurseries for domestic consumption. This is a sport best left to the knowledgeable.

These plants may not be widely available, but they are a fascinating lot and worth looking for. If you can't find any, join a rock garden society. They have wonderful seed exchanges and good information about how to grow from seed easily.

Keith Squires' Scree

Nurseryman Keith Squires has created some of the most amazing scree gardens I've seen (see shot #16). His busy season coincides with the growing season of his plants. He devised this surefire method of planting. The results are extraordinary.

He uses a Granular A stone, and the bed contains no soil at all except what's attached to the plants' roots in transplanting. No weeding is necessary, and it attracts no slugs at all (the surface is too difficult for those soft, slimy bodies). It was planted in July 1992 and has neither been watered, depending only on the natural rainfall, nor fertilized.

Squires grows the following in a space 20 feet long, 4 feet wide and 18 inches deep.

Front row, left to right: *Erigeron; Orostachys Boehmeria; Veronica schmidtiana; Arabis procumbens; Antennaria dioica; Sedum cauticola* 'Roseum.'

Center left: *Draba bryoides imbricata; Sempervivum* 'Compte de Congai.'

Left: *Silene schafta.*

Rear: *Arenaria* 'Bevans.'

More plants for the scree from Keith Squires' list of excellent scree plants: *Potentilla x tonguei; Campanula kemulariae; Achillea kolbiana; Allium cyathophorum* var. *farreri; Allium mairei; Aurinia saxatilis* 'Dudley Neville'; *Aruncus aethusifolius; Aster tibeticus; Campanula carpatica* 'E.H. Frost.'

Plants for Sunny Slopes

Acantholimon, Onosma, Asperula, Draba (be careful— they are susceptible to mildew and rot).

Plants for Shade

Most alpines need a sunny open spot, with the exception of the following: *Ramonda, Haberlea,* some *Primula* spp., *Cassiope, Gaultheria* and *Vaccinium,* which likes a cool north aspect.

ROCK GARDEN TIPS

✦ A bit of advice about actually making a small rock garden: Don't let the rocks stick up like sentinels; bury them to a depth of at least half to two-thirds so they seem to be pushing up from the soil. Make the strata or striations in the rock point in one direction; again, this gives it the semblance of having been left behind by a glacier. Look at the wonderful arrangement of rocks and plants in

Larry Davidson's garden (see shot #18).

✦ A rock garden can look pretty awful because it's not a simple thing to design, and once in place, you aren't going to change it easily. Use rocks that are in scale with your site. Having huge stones in a tiny space won't leave you much room for plants, and it will overwhelm with its demands. Make sure there are lots of little nooks and crannies to put plants into.

✦ You can introduce scree into the rock garden using any of the mixes above. Just make sure you have a mix of 60 percent grit, gravel or rock chips; 20 percent soil and leaf mold. You can do even leaner mixes than this with up to 80 percent grit.

✦ Prep the site properly. Take out all weeds. You can do this by solarizing the space by covering it with heavy black plastic, a drop sheet or anything else you can weigh down with rocks or bricks. Leave it for a couple of weeks. Most of the weeds will expire by the time you lift the lid. You can use a weed killer such as Roundup to finish things off. Usually I haven't found this necessary in a small location. It's important to get all the weed root systems out. Alpines simply won't stand up to the competition. In their natural location, they have none.

✦ Remove leaves and other bits of garden detritus where slugs and friends can hang out. This should be a fairly clean area, which means don't site it under a tree. I've done that, and it's nonstop work and fuss. Of course, I think that's kind of fun.

✦ To keep up the vitality of the bed, whip out anything that looks sick or sad. Move the ailing ones to a nursery spot, and replace with fresh new plants, putting them in with lots of water and tenderness.

Rock Garden Maintenance

✦ Clean up in fall or early spring, when plants are dormant. Top-dress with leaf mold and coarse sharp sand or $3/8$-inch gravel. Foster recommends adding a handful of manure and bonemeal to each bushel.

✦ If you decide to water, do so on cool, windy days, and water long and deep. Don't do this unless it's absolutely necessary and the plants are wilting even in early morning.

CRACKS AND CREVICES

In the search for new spots to garden in, no place, however unpromising, should be overlooked. Plants on their own will find almost any site—a crack in the sidewalk, a perch on a cliff, stuffed beside a riser on a stone walk—so there's good reason to imitate nature wherever possible in these spots.

Your gardening tools and sensibility have to shift downward. A teaspoon may be more useful than a favorite trowel. And though you think it's dead simple to get these things going—look at the weeds growing between the patio bricks—it's a lot more difficult than it appears. It may take years and years, maybe even decades, for a few seeds to establish themselves on a cliff. You want them to germinate as soon as possible.

Many plants love the warmth of stone and rock. Their root systems will burrow deeply into the soil under the rock for protection, the good drainage usually found here and the nutrients provided by the rock. If you try pulling one of these out a few years down the road, you'll be astounded at the steadfastness and length of the root system.

You also have to keep in mind how big the plants will get in a couple of years and not plant a cascader above one that likes to stay in a neat little bun. The latter will get swamped. For instance, plants such as aubrieta, arabis, dianthus or cerastium will hang down a couple of feet in a few years and will threaten any other plants living below them.

To get plants established in the most unlikely places, try the following:

+ To get seeds into place, fold a piece of cardboard or stiff paper index card in half, put the seeds in the fold, and blow them into the soil mix in the crevice. Use a fine spray until the seeds germinate. Beware of letting seeds and soil wash out by rain or hose.
+ Make sure you prep the area under the cracks, stones or crevices as widely as possible so the roots will have room to spread out. This may be under stones where it will be cool.

In Amy and Clair Stewart's garden (see shot #17), you can see a beautifully constructed stone wall with plants spilling down the side. As the wall was being built, pockets of soil were left intact just for the positioning of plants and then hanging plants were inserted into them.

Gravel Gardening

This is a form of gardening that has become, for want of a better word, hot. It is the definitive xeriscape garden, which means using plants that need as little water as possible.

If you have a pocket that you want to turn into a gravel garden, the easiest method is to remove all the soil down to about 8 inches and see what you are dealing with. Fast-draining soil will be ideal for a gravel garden. Any area that allows water to sit about or linger for a long time will need more digging. Make sure the area is level so that you don't get water pooling or washing out during a storm.

Add a layer of horticultural sand. Backfill with gravel, such as the screening Keith Squires mentions, and then top-dress with pea gravel for looks. I've seen this kind of gardening done with river stone, which is very expensive but looks sensational.

Choose plants that like a fast-draining situation and won't need constant watering. Place plants in groups that have exactly the same kind of light and water needs. Mediterranean herbs such as rosemary, thyme and lavender, for instance, would look perfect together.

As would any number of ornamental grasses. The plants will survive on the soil they are planted with, nutrition from the rocks and what water nature supplies.

Pockets in Walls or Steps

✦ The major difficulty here is getting plants to stay in place without drying up or falling out. If you have enough grass, cut out a section of turf, and roll up the little plant in the turf, jellyroll fashion. Soak the roll, shove it into the crevice, and soak again.

Planting in Steps

✦ Put plants in place to figure out what goes where. Shoehorn the plants into place with a large spoon or small transplanting trowel. Firm the soil around the plants with your fingers, and water with a mister, making sure that the roots are well soaked.

PLANT SUGGESTIONS

✦ Curry plant, *Helichrysum angustifolium*; pineapple mint, *Mentha suaveolens* 'Variegata'; Corsican mint, *M. requienii*; dwarf blue fescue grass, *Festuca glauca*; deadnettle, *Lamium maculatum* 'White Nancy'; silver thyme; various coral bells, *Heuchera*; tiarellas; *Nicotiana sylvestris*, a tall, slim plant that will self-sow; *Corydalis lutea* (self-sows); *Alchemilla alpina*; baby's breath, *Gypsophila repens*; white pansies; baby's tears, *Helxine soleirolii*; *Sedum floriferum* 'Weihenstephaner Gold'; *S. sieboldii*; dianthus; draba, saxifrages, androsaces and raoulia; violets; *Silene maritima*; and succulents such as echeverias.

14

Gloria Bishop's balcony is a splendid example of how to turn a dull space into something that's both exciting and visually stimulating. See page 127 for details.

15

Marjorie Harris' sidewalk retrieval contains a mix of plants with a variety of foliage, shapes and colors. Lavender provides a basis as an edger. See page 137.

10

Water Gardening

All gardens, no matter how small, must have water. It's an element we need profoundly, especially in cramped urban spaces. There's something almost hypnotic, infinitely soothing about the movement of water, and it's becoming a necessity when you consider how noisy our towns and cities have become. Water can also be a focal point in a postage-stamp-sized garden without being pretentious.

Water can be had inexpensively. A pot, a tub or even a jardinière can be host to a small, bubbling fountain. It's the sound and the movement that's important. You can buy already-assembled stones with a circulating pump installed and all you have to do is arrange the rocks provided.

But if you have a good eye, putting together the elements yourself can be done without a lot of fuss. Any container will do, and if you like the idea of water tumbling over rocks, head for a quarry. It's like going to the stone store, where you can find all sorts of gorgeous forms. The only inhibition is the size and weight of the stones that will fit in a car or van.

The circulating pump will have to be underwater and the pipe hidden. The only other things you'll need are an electrical outlet and the occasional topping up with water to have a really good little water feature with a minimum of effort and expense.

Water can be had in the most amazing small spaces. I have a big old tub that sits on a ledge under a mirror with the head of a lion embedded in it.

It started out with water dripping from the lion's mouth. I found out just how important the sound is the minute I turned it on. My neighbor said it was like a leaky toilet. Not exactly what I had in mind. No amount of rearranging stone or cutting down the size of the thrust of water seemed to improve it. A change to a bubbling fountain made everyone happy, including my grandchildren, who can spend hours examining water dripping over their hands in the sunlight.

I planted it up with grasses and duckweed, which lasted until the raccoons discovered it—about a week. They trashed the plants, flinging them all over the deck. Careful replacement didn't stop them for a moment. Draping mesh over the works lasted a couple of nights. I finally gave up.

Now, the simple circulating pump operates alone and does the job for which it was intended: to mask the sound of the ever-present buzzing of machines and lawn mowers. It also puts me in a nice, dreamy mood, just hearing the sound of water babbling. In fact, I like the whole effect so much, I bring the pump indoors in winter, put it into an attractive, glazed pot and let it murmur away.

There are small, decorative fountains with mini-pumps that drip water prettily which can be set into or on a wall. These are ideal for balconies or tiny spaces outside a window or door.

If you look at shot #3, you'll see a front garden with a fountain. It's really a very large concrete bowl with a circulating pump, but what an effect it has—it gives a miniature space real presence.

Here are some tips on bringing water into the garden:

+ Sink a precast form into the garden, edge it with attractive stones, and position a very small pump for circulation and sound.

+ Dig a hole and install a child's pool painted a dark color. Edge with flat stones. Be sure that there is an electrical outlet close by for a small, self-circulating fountain.

+ Take an old porcelain sink (which can still be found in junkyards)—put in a stopper to keep it water-tight—or a stone or metal trough, even a large jardinière without a hole in the bottom, and add a water lily, a water hyacinth and a few other plants, such as duckweed, to keep the water clean.

✦ A traditional gargoyle mounted on a wall with a hose behind and a circulating pump in a small container below can enhance a small formal garden.

CREATING AN ECOSYSTEM

If you want a true pond, you'll need a variety of plants to create a self-sustaining ecosystem: cleaners, oxygenators and shade-givers. Flowering plants will need about six hours of sun a day, which is why you also need plants to cast some shade on the water. This will make it cool enough to discourage algae from forming. Plants will need water at least 18 to 24 inches deep with about 18 square feet of space. This may outlaw such a pool in your pocket garden, or it could become a pocket garden in itself.

I'd go for any of the following water gardens in a container as a substitute for native ponds or bogs, tempting as they are. As I keep saying, it's the sound and the movement that are important in a tiny garden. And the wonderful thing about a pond in a pot is that you won't have to worry about watering plants, and it will become a magnet for birds, bees and any other insect to take a drink on parching summer days.

A few caveats about any water feature:

✦ Make sure the container is level, or it will drive you crazy because the water will most certainly be level and make everything else look askew.

+ Keep it away from trees as much as possible to cut down on the amount of work retrieving fallen leaves, which would muck up the water.
+ When adding water, make sure it has been sitting long enough to get rid of chemicals and that the temperature is about the same as the container's.

A Half-Barrel Water Garden

I'm suggesting a half-barrel here, but you can substitute almost any form of holder you can imagine, from a plastic barrel to an antique trough. No matter what you choose, it's going to end up being extremely heavy, so have it in its final resting place before you start filling it with water. For instance, a gallon of water weighs about 8 pounds.

+ Clean the container carefully, scrubbing the interior with soap and water. Fill and empty several times to remove any residue. Then fill and leave for several days for the wood to swell and make it leakproof.
+ Paint the metal with a rust-resistant finish. If there is any leakage, line with one of the excellent thick, black plastic liners on the market—just staple it to the edges.
+ Add a circulating pump, or if you decide to add plants, try the following:
+ Add 5 inches of soil; 1 inch of sand (this is to hold the soil down); fill the tub with water, and let it

warm up naturally by the sun for a day or two. This will also get rid of many of the chemicals we have in the local tap water.

✦ Water lilies need water at least 2 feet deep. They need six hours of sun and bloom in July. Plant the roots and rhizomes in the soil; tie oxygenators in a loose bundle and attach to the bottom with a stone.

✦ Don't let anyone stir it up; fertilize with tablets shoved into the soil around plants.

✦ Fish add interest and help curb the mosquito population. They aren't absolutely necessary, but if you do keep them, each fish will need 8 gallons of water. Move them indoors for the winter; frogs will hibernate outdoors.

✦ To overwinter hardy plants, bury them in a sheltered spot; or put in a cold place that doesn't freeze.

A DOUBLE-BARREL WATERFALL

Temma Gentles and Victor Levin are next-door neighbors whose front pocket garden is shown in shot #4. In what is now a mutual backyard, they share a two-barrel fountain-cum-waterfall that is not only an effective sound system to mask out the noise from a busy road nearby but also an attractive and necessary demarcation between the two properties since they took down the fence.

A shopping trip to a water nursery unearthed preformed liners that work perfectly inside whisky barrels (they already had two of them). They bought the smallest circulating pump available and some plants.

First, they dug two holes, one deeper than the other so that the barrels would be on different levels. They dug down far enough to accommodate each one at the halfway level, then poured sand into the holes. A 2-by-2-foot patio stone was placed in the bottom of each of the holes and made level on the sand.

The preforms were put inside the barrels, and holes were drilled in the barrels (and preforms) to shove the pipe from the pump in the bottom barrel through to the top barrel. To make the holes watertight, silicone sealer was applied around the edges of the pipe. Then both outside holes were backfilled with pea gravel and sand so that no dirt would touch the barrels and cause them to rot.

The electrical wire was run from the pump to the house and covered with rocks. Rocks also become the waterfall from one level to the other—piled up in the bottom barrel so the water could run over them. Gentles and Levin found they became sound engineers. The argument on one side was to have Niagara Falls cutting off all traffic noise; on the other, to have a soft, romantic trickle. They've ended up with a compromise. The trick, says Levin, is to have a stone with a concave hollow in it for the water to splash over to get the most convincing and pleasing sound.

They keep the motor on all the time, going on the theory that it will be easier on the motor than turning it on and off. They also planted papyrus and other water plants that have attracted raccoons every night. One solution is to throw plastic netting over it at the end of the day. The battle continues.

To give the surround a natural look, they planted *Cimicifuga racemosa* and *Peltiphyllum peltatum* (which is known as *Dammera* and commonly called umbrella plant because it can get so big).

BALCONY WATER FOUNTAIN

Even the tiniest balcony can support a fountain. On the balcony featured on the cover, Gloria Bishop now has a fountain among her wonderful collection of pots. She found a large pot about 2 feet in diameter without a hole in the bottom and added a selection of magnificent stones and pieces of crystal that she's collected over the years. They are used to prop up and anchor a terra-cotta birdbath in the middle. This was an artifact picked up in Cyprus, but the birds never seemed attracted to it. It's a bell-like piece of terra-cotta with a knob on top to hang the bath, and a protruding lip in which to put water at one side.

The top knob and the side lip were knocked off. A tiny 2-by-2-inch circulating pump was placed inside the bell. Rubber tubing runs from the pump to the hole in the top and water now splashes up and over the side. The sound can be heard throughout the apartment and it cuts down the noise from the nearby streets. She has to top up the water occasionally, but that's about it for maintenance.

She's even been able to add a few plants: papyrus, duckweed and water lettuce, which keep the water sparkling clean. Using the terra-cotta for the container and the interior bell makes the fountain fit in with the collection of pots that grace the whole of the balcony. And, of course, she doesn't have to deal with raccoons, squirrels or mosquitoes.

SOME WATER PLANTS

Plant up containers in June, when things have warmed up completely. Floating plants will provide shelter for fish, prevent algae and are easy to keep under control. Oxygenating water weeds will act as an understory. Just remember not to put in too many plants. This is definitely not the place for intensive planting. The rule of thumb for water gardeners is to use one plant for every square yard of water surface plus four bunches of oxygenators. Go for the hardiest type of plants rather than exotics. They may winter over and will take less space.

Cabomba caroliniana, cabomba, is an oxygenator that helps control algae; light green, fan-shaped leaves grow stems 12 to 18 inches long. Needs still water.

Cyperus spp., papyrus, has an almost Oriental look to it, so if it's your intention to have a meditation garden, this plant is a must. Needs either damp soil or at least 6 inches of water.

Eichhornia crassipes, water hyacinth. Its floating roots will filter water, and it has a lavender, orchidlike bloom. Needs three hours of sun a day. It's known to control algae.

Elodea canadensis is the best known of the oxygenators and looks a bit like seaweed. It can be invasive so should be planted in a container before being submerged.

Hygrophila polysperma, red hygrophila, is an oxygenator with thick green leaves, but it isn't hardy.

Lemna minor, duckweed, is the tiniest of all plants and will cover the surface of the pond. If you have goldfish, they'll eat it up.

Nelumbo spp., lotus, 'Chawan Basu,' is a white-flowered, semi-dwarf lotus; 'Momo Botan' is even smaller, with leaves 10 to 18 inches across. Needs full sun, and grows by creeping rhizomes.

Nuphar pumilum, yellow pond lily, is small, can adapt to light shade and needs water 18 to 40 inches deep.

Nymphaea spp., water lilies, come in hardy and exotic forms. The hardy ones, such as *N.* 'Virginalis,' will winter over. Exotics have larger blooms and heady scent. 'James Brydon' is a subtle beauty. They need full sun with from 18 to 36 inches of water. The floating leaves provide shade.

Sagittaria, arrowhead, is another oxgenator. Look for the dwarf version. It spreads by runners and has arrow-shaped leaves.

Sarracenia spp., pitcher plant, has modified leaves with hooded tops, forming pitchers.

11

Favorite Pocket Plants

Gardening may be trendy and it may be about attitude, but mostly it's about plants. Since I started gardening in little pockets many years ago, I've built up a prejudice about plants. I love most of them, but I do admit that some are more appropriate than others when it comes to pocket gardening.

What follows is not meant to be comprehensive. It's filled with personal choices, and there are plants I haven't touched at all that may be proper. My omissions are on purpose—I probably haven't grown the plants, or they are just so common that they don't need to be recorded here. I've included more woody plants than any other because I think these are the hardest to choose from. Scale is really important here, so keep in mind that none of these plants is monumental.

Here are some principles to keep in mind when you are choosing plants for a pocket garden:

+ Don't be afraid to experiment with putting many elements together. You can be much looser in the choices for a large space than you can in a small space, where careful thought is given as to how many plants you put in.
+ Take it easy on using a wild number of diverse, variegated plants. Much as I love them, too many in a confined space is really unattractive. The same can be said for brilliant gold or large-leaved plants. One or two of these in a very small space is a visual relief rather than an overwhelming statement.
+ Work out a palette. It doesn't matter if it's soft pastel tones or brilliant colors. Hot gardens can be just as effective in a small space as in a larger one.

A Few Tips on Using Plants

+ Pale flowers with dark leaves or against a dark background of another plant give the impression of space between them, especially at night. The lighter colors will appear to come forward as the others retreat.
+ Always surround garden artifacts by plants so that they are partially hidden.
+ Don't be afraid to have large plants in the foreground, with small plants receding into the background. This will add the illusion of depth.

✦ Always fill the garden with little surprises, such as going past a shrub or small tree to find another plant arrangement or a secret place to sit.

✦ Place favorite small objects among the plants. A shell here, a glass bauble there, a special stone someone has given you will delight your guests.

Espalier is a very old-fashioned way of dealing with lots of plants in little space. Some excellent books on the subject are available, and if you decide to do something ambitious, get some training. If you want to experiment, try the following: The idea is to take a shrub or dwarf fruit tree and train it along wires. This can be used as a divider in a small garden, or it can be done even more effectively up against a fence. The warmth of the background will mean that you can develop tender fruit even if you live in a harsh climate. Choose the form you want to emulate (candelabra, chevrons, parallel wires). Have the background (strong wires anchored to the shape you have in mind) in place before you plant. Plant the shrub or vine in the center. Use the leader to define the shape, and cut everything else away except where you want to train the branches along wires. This is labor-intensive, and you have to prune regularly.

MAINTENANCE

Keep uppermost in your mind that small spaces can be planted intensively, and the more you plant the more they are likely to duke it out for themselves without a lot of worry and fussing from you. They will drop their own litter, which will feed the soil and keep them healthy.

✦ Find something small to clear off detritus when it becomes too deep. I used an old pair of leather gloves to dust things off but more recently found that a children's wooden leaf rake helps pull things away from plants without damaging them.

✦ Let fallen leaves lie. Think like a forest, where litter is left as it falls. Cut back as few plants as possible. Leave them as forage for birds, and the dead stems will protect the plant during the winter. Spring is the time for cleaning up.

✦ Containers are another matter: Plants in pots don't mind crowded conditions, but you have to watch them carefully for watering needs. I have a routine with my containers and stick to it: Get up early, have coffee watching the sun come into the garden, and water the containers. I usually leave water sitting overnight to get rid of any chemicals and keep it at the same temperature as the air around.

FAVORITE POCKET PLANTS

What follows are some of the plants I particularly like to tuck into small places. There are many, many more, and if you are a regular at a good nursery, you should be able to get excellent advice.

WOODY PLANTS

This category covers a huge range of plants. Here, I'm sticking to small trees and shrubs. These are the plants to get in place right at the beginning of your garden design. They become the bones of the garden and give it substance. My advice is always to buy small, let it acclimatize to the site, and you'll end up with a plant that will be a lot happier than going for something grand just for an immediate effect.

Planting Tips

+ Plant bare-root plants in the spring. Mulch after planting.
+ Dig a hole as deep as the roots of the shrub and at least three times as wide as the rootball. Settle the plant in with the "face" where you can see it. This is tricky, but walk around the shrub or tree several times, and you'll be able to see its best side. That's the one you want to face. Water the bottom of the hole to check for drainage; settle in the plant; and backfill with unamended soil. I do this so that the root system doesn't go into shock when it reaches the periphery of amended soil. Then top-dress the hole with a generous lashing of compost or well-composted manure; mulch with a combination of compost, manure and cocofiber in equal parts.
+ Water a couple of times a week for the first season. Do it deeply, and do it in the morning, making sure

you don't get water on the plant's leaves (to avoid burning by the sun).

Trees

Look for small trees that will keep their height to 25 feet or less. It's not fair to plant a monster tree and keep it trimmed down to your needs. Find the right tree for your space. If you grow on a mound or a berm, get a tree with deep roots, such as a ginkgo. In a pocket garden, most maples with their shallow feeder roots aren't going to be the best choice. But all of the following will do beautifully in a small space.

Amelanchier canadensis, serviceberry, grows to about 20 feet, has the most glorious white blooms in spring and makes a leafy bower; a superb screening plant which offers no problems that I've seen over the 30-year life of the one in my own garden. Nothing bothers this plant.

Acer palmatum 'Sango Kaku' or 'Senkaki,' coralbark maple, is not supposed to be particularly hardy. But I'm in Zone 6b, and it's wintered over beautifully for many years in front of a north-facing fence. It is out of the wind, and I do feed it compost. The red bark is magnificent. *A. griseum*, paperbark maple, will make a lovely winter statement. *A. ginnala*, Amur maple, grows to 30 feet, has white flowers in summer and turns bright red in autumn.

Betula nana, dwarf birch, is a pretty little plant. It comes out very late in spring, sometimes close to summer. But the wait is worth it. *B. nigra*, river birch, is a native North American that is far less susceptible to birch borer and bronze borer than are other species and grows slowly to 30 feet. Of course, the white bark looks smashing in the winter.

Cercidiphyllum japonicum, katsura, an underused tree with heart-shaped leaves. The bark goes shaggy in old age, but it's the spreading form and the leaf shape that are this tree's glory. The foliage starts out a reddish purple color and turns a gorgeous pale hue in autumn. The species can get to 60 feet and up, but *c. j.* 'Pendulum' grows to 25 feet.

Cercis canadensis, Eastern redbud, has glorious red beads in spring and a lovely heart-shaped leaf. 'Forest Pansy' has reddish purple leaves and is one of the most striking of all small trees. To 30 feet.

Cornus alternifolia, pagoda dogwood, is a marvelous little tree with a charming horizontal shape. *C. controversa* 'Argentea' is an even more striking form. *C. alba* 'Elegantissima' has variegated leaves and will grow madly in the shade, though becoming a little leggy. This is one that needs pruning for shape on a regular basis. Gorgeous.

Cotinus coggygria, purple smoketree or smoke bush, has a rounded purple leaf that is fantastic as a background color for so many plants that you can almost plan around this one as a specimen. The flowers puff out and create a smoky, ethereal effect. From 15 feet.

Elaeagnus angustifolia, Russian olive. Heavy-duty

silver foliage, grows to 30 feet, but it reacts to pruning very well and looks very dramatic. A bit messy in late spring, but, no matter, this is a good little tree. It is salt-tolerant.

Ginkgo biloba, maidenhair tree. The fan-shaped leaves of this tree are so graceful that I have to peer at them every day. Check out the bark on a winter's day, and you'll find that this plant is still warm to the touch. Gets to 50 feet but it is elegant. Buy a male tree (the fruit from the female tends to be smelly and messy); salt- and pollution-tolerant. Fall color is radiant gold.

Koelreuteria paniculata, golden-rain tree. Long, serrated leaves, rounded form with yellow panicles in July.

Malus 'Red Jade,' flowering crab apple. Blooms open white from deep pink buds; the cherry-red fruit stays on until December, or birds get to them. Weeping, grows to 15 feet. There are hundreds of cultivars. Find one that isn't susceptible to fire blight and scab.

Prunus sargentii, Sargent cherry, grows to 30 feet, has early-spring flowers of blush pink and shiny, dark green leaves.

Pyrus salicifolia 'Pendula' is another of those little trees that I had to have once I saw it elsewhere. The silver of the leaves alone (even more intense in a form named 'Argentea') is worth having. It really needs superb drainage, so I have it bermed on top of sand

and gravel. It should be out of the wind, but I didn't have a choice with this one. It's fine. Needs a warm, dry site.

Salix integra 'Hakuro-nishiki,' variegated willow. You might think I'm mad to suggest a willow for a very small garden, but this one is an exception. Early new leaves are bright shrimp-pink, changing to cream and white. Grows to about 15 feet, but can be cut to the ground every spring.

Sambucus canadensis is a great 12-foot plant. The golden form, *S. c.* 'Aurea,' needs cutting back each year to retain the gold of its leaves. Birds love this small tree. I also like the variegated form.

Shrubs

Check out the size and mass of shrubs desired. Imagine the overall effect rather than singling out any one plant. Don't shove them in too close together, especially in a pocket garden; a little space will give you a less strained and crowded feeling. It may take three years, but they will mass together in that time. It's important to check out pruning time when you make your purchase. Then prune out dead wood and crossed branches in spring. Leave spring bloomers alone until they've finished flowering.

Acanthopanax sieboldianus. Prickly, a good edger to keep out dogs and children from a small garden. Lends itself very nicely to pruning as a hedge. Needs nothing much but pruning for shape and will take shade.

Buddleia davidii, butterfly bush, is a tricky plant in anything colder than Zone 6. It gets killed right back, but don't give up on it in spring—it tends to come out late. Try *B. lochinch*, which is a much hardier type for those who just can't seem to grow *B. davidii* hybrids. Late to start, but it also keeps on blooming until frost. Mulch deeply in fall, and don't disturb until late spring.

Buxus microphylla, littleleaf boxwood. There are so many hybrid forms that it's worthwhile searching out one that's hardy to your area. They need little work and can be pruned back late in May for shape. Use as a hedge or even as a specimen. I love them in winter, since they hold a light fall of snow so gracefully.

Caryopteris x clandonensis, bluebeard, is such a useful shrub that I can't imagine being without it. It tends to be a bit slow in unfurling its silvery leaves in spring and has blue flowers in summer. Don't cut it back too early in spring. Prune for shape only.

Clethra alnifolia, summersweet, comes in both white and pink forms. Though it is slow to come out in spring, don't despair; it will have lovely blooms in August, when almost everything else looks blah. Good in semi-shade.

Cornus spp. There are so many good dogwoods for small gardens, you can have a great selection even among my own favorites: *C. alba* 'Sibirica' is great because of the red stems in winter. Grows quickly to its full 10 feet in height. *C. a.* 'Argenteo-marginata' has silver-edged leaves that are gorgeous in a shady spot. Be careful of *C. sericea,* red osier dogwood: It's a traveler and has no place in a tiny garden. *C. florida* has a nasty reputation for developing insects and diseases. With a middling amount of sun and lots of compost, I've had no problems.

Daphne x burkwoodii, daphne. What a great group this is, with well-formed vase shapes and scented blooms in late spring and again in autumn. I love *D. x b.* 'Carol Mackie' and 'Silver Edge,' both of which have lovely margins and white to pink blooms. A new one that should be a treasure is 'Brigg's Moonlight.' It has golden yellow, rounded leaves and an acid-green edging. I've grown daphnes from little sticks a few inches high to 5-foot beauties. They hang on to their leaves almost all winter in Zone 6b.

Elsholtzia stauntonii, mint shrub. A nice little shrub that grows to 5 feet and has a minty scent, dark green leaves and purply flowers in summer and early fall.

Enkianthus campanulatus has a slender profile that fits right into the pocket garden. It grows to 6 to 8 feet, and has wee, pink-striated bells; its strong, small leaves turn a magnificent deep flame orange to magenta in autumn. It prefers acid soil, but I grow it in well-drained clay with lots of compost, moisture and a bit of shade.

Exochorda x macrantha, dwarf pearlbush. No problems with this one, and its lovely, slightly weeping form makes it a winner. 'The Bride' blooms for about six weeks. Put it with something else that turns brilliant in fall, as this one is a bit boring at that time.

Fothergilla gardenii is a dwarf form of *F. major*. It has the most gorgeous autumn color imaginable and pretty white fuzzy-looking blooms at the end of the stem in spring. I don't grow it on acid soil (which it is supposed to prefer), and it's just fine. This form grows to about 3 feet in sun or shade; mulch well.

Hydrangea paniculata 'Grandiflora,' PeeGee hydrangea, is ideal for a show all summer long. I like this form, with its pure white, lacecap flowers, rather than the big, old-fashioned mophead blooms. When planting, cut back to about five stems. Blooms on new wood; prune in late fall or winter. Height variable up to 15 feet. 'Tardiva' is especially attractive, blooms for weeks on end and grows to 9 feet. *H. quercifolia*, oak-leaf hydrangea, is among my favs with exfoliating bark and lovely green leaves that turn a gorgeous deep red in autumn; the lacecap blooms turn a pale pink. Use this one alone, and you won't regret it. I have found no problems, and it survives in semi-shade. It can grow to 6 feet.

Ilex crenata 'Compacta,' Japanese holly, has a nice rounded form about 6 feet high. Evergreen and barely needs pruning. *I. glabra*, inkberry, is a great little plant. Its wonderful, shiny, black-green leaves stay that way all winter long. Normally, it's a bog plant, but I've got it in ordinary soil in a really protected spot and mulch it deeply. It's come through a couple of winters very well indeed. If it gets leggy, prune hard. Might sucker.

Itea virginica, Virginia sweetspire, is sort of ever-green, which means that it looks good until midwinter, then turns yucky. But it will grow in awful clay, has drooping white flowers in spring and grows to about 4 feet. Has wonderful red foliage.

Kalmia latifolia, mountain laurel. A great evergreen shrub. This is one that proves my point about buying small and letting them acclimatize. I bought a tiny one, plunked it on a berm, added soil all around, then mulched with pine needles. It finally rewarded me with enchanting pink flowers. Dozens of cultivars with white to dark pink or red blooms.

Magnolia stellata, star magnolia. An utterly charm-ing spring shrub that won't get too large for our purposes—it grows to 15 feet and has striking blooms in May that come out before the dark green leaves.

Mahonia aquifolium, Oregon grape. It is, hands-down, one of the best winter plants for a cold climate. A really tough plant that looks a little like a holly with bright shiny green leaves all summer; in autumn it turns an almost burnished magenta and stays that way all winter. Its one drawback is that, in early spring, it looks dreadful for several weeks. Resist the temptation to either prune it or yank it out. It will slowly come back from the stems with a pale green leaf. Requires no work except to prune for shape.

Myrica pensylvanica, bayberry, is almost evergreen in Zone 6b, which means the lovely, stiff, deep green leaves will stay on the branches most of the winter and then suddenly turn brown. It's slow to start in spring, so it must be accompanied with something that unfurls early (dwarf lilac; *Kerria japonica* 'Picta'; or *Viburnum plicatum* 'Summer Snowflake').

Pieris japonica 'Mountain Fire' grows to 9 feet, is evergreen and has the most enchanting, brilliant red growth in spring. It can get right out of hand in ideal conditions (acid soil, with lots of humus in part shade). In less-than-ideal conditions, it will stay relatively small and is a good berm plant.

Rhododendron. Try a few of the smaller forms of very hardy rhododendrons if you have the right conditions—woodland, no aggressive competition from the roots of the other plants. *R. ramapo* is a charming little species with tiny purple blooms. 'Aglo' has rosy-pink flowers; 'PJM' leaves turn a reddish color in winter, blooms lavender-pink.

Salix caprea 'Pendula,' weeping goat willow, is a low-growing shrub that reaches about 1 foot but could reach 5 or 6 feet, depending on the location. If you love silvery catkins, this is a great spring plant.

Syringa, lilac. The Korean hybrids are dwarf forms ideal for a pocket garden. 'Miss Kim' is the most widely used. *S. velutina* and *S. reticulata* are two other forms that should be checked out, since they bloom later than *S. vulgaris* and they grow to about 8 feet. (Some encyclopedias give various heights: *velutina* from 5 to 10 feet, *reticulata* 30 feet, but this will depend on how severe your weather is. Check with a good local grower.)

Viburnum spp. are my favorite of all plants. They look good all year, and each one has its own personality. I've never had a problem, except when they've been placed poorly (by me). Here's a few of the smaller ones: *V. plicatum* 'Shasta' has a fine horizontal form that's smothered with pale cream blooms in spring; *V. p.* 'Summer Snowflake' is smaller and has lacecap blooms that start in June and seem to go on for months. This one is easy to prune for shape and site.

Evergreen Plants

Abies balsamea 'Nana,' dwarf balsam fir, or *A. concolor* 'Compacta,' dwarf white fir. Shallow roots, but need well-drained soil. Can take shade.

Andromeda polifolia, bog rosemary. Glossy green leaves, pink flowers in spring. Needs acid soil and sun. Grows to 2 feet.

Chamaecyparis obtusa 'Nana,' dwarf Hinoki false cypress, needs sun and rich, well-drained soil out of the wind. Grows to 3 feet.

Daphne cneorum, rose daphne or garland flower. Dark green all year, makes a good groundcover and can take a little shade. Grows up to 1 foot with a spread of 2 feet.

Picea glauca 'Albertiana Conica,' dwarf Alberta spruce. Light green, conical, grows to 12 feet over a long time.

Pinus mugo 'Compacta,' dwarf mugo pine. Grows to 5 feet; dense rounded shape.

Taxus, yew. Deep black-green, almost unkillable. It's the garden's best backdrop plant. I like to put red-stalked plants such as Siberian dogwood or coralbark maple in front. For my money, yews can be used anywhere in the garden where a small statement is needed or winter interest is necessary. Few things are more ravishing than a well-kept yew hedge.

Thuja occidentalis 'Globosa,' grows up to 6 feet with a round form and gray-green foliage.

Tsuga, hemlock, is a gorgeous family of evergreens. *T. caroliniana* 'Compacta' is low-growing and dense and responds to pruning.

Vines

Once the trees and shrubs are in place, get the vines in. Like papering or painting the walls of any room, you wouldn't leave it until last.

It's difficult to do the following the first time round, but believe me, it makes for a much tougher plant: Prune it hard once you've planted it the first year. After that, do normal pruning in March or April, and train the vine up a support.

Ampelopsis brevipedunculata 'Elegans,' variegated porcelain vine, is a form with pink and white splashes on the leaves and the most glorious turquoise to purple berries in autumn. Might seed around.

Clematis spp. is the most valuable of all vines for a small garden. They will flower from spring to autumn if you get a selection. *C. texensis, C. alpina* are among the early-flowering species. *C. virginiana* (a.k.a. Virgin's bower) is a little too rampant for most pocket gardens but looks lovely. *C. macropetala* and *C. integrifolia* are both worth looking into. Shrubby forms such as *C. stans* and *C. recta* have blue and white blooms, respectively. *C. terniflora,* sweet autumn clematis, is a fast traveler, but any garden will be enhanced by the white flowers and sweet smell.

Ipomoea batatas 'Blackie,' black sweet potato vine. Let the dramatic black, deeply lobed leaves hang over the edge of a pot or climb a wall in sharp contrast with the gray or silver foliage of other plants. Considered an annual and worthwhile putting in every year.

Schizophragma hydrangeoides, Japanese hydrangea vine, is fairly hard to find but will become increasingly popular because it is so fantastic. It's a self-clinger that travels at a slow pace and doesn't get all blowsy. Lovely lacecap flowers from early summer to autumn, when they turn a burnished bronze. Requires no work.

Hydrangea petiolaris, climbing hydrangea, is slow to start, but, like ivy, once it starts to move, it gallops. Gets very blowsy when it begins to bloom. After flowers are spent, cut back to keep it under control. Be brutal—this plant can really get out of hand.

Lonicera x brownii 'Dropmore Scarlet,' honeysuckle. Red flowers start in June and carry right on until frost. Very hardy.

Parthenocissus quinquefolia, Virginia creeper, is ubiquitous, and the main reasons to grow it are that birds need it for forage, the autumn color is smashing and it looks like tangled lace in winter.

Pyracantha coccinea, scarlet firethorn, which can also be espaliered along wire, has bright red blooms followed by shiny red to orange berries. The spread on this plant is about 8 feet by 10 feet and smaller in areas colder than Zone 6.

Solanum jasminoides 'Album Variegatum,' variegated potato vine. In most zones except the warmest, this would be considered an annual.

GRASSES

Ornamental grasses will last right through the year looking good. Just whack them back to a couple of inches in spring, and they will start new growth immediately. Grasses have the virtue of sounding good as well as looking good in the winter. There are a few heavy-duty spreaders, but I've left them out. All of these are well-behaved additions to any garden or container.

Andropogon scoparius, little bluestem, takes any soil, produces fluffy white heads. Incredible fall color—turns almost red and stays that way.

Chasmanthium latifolium, Northern sea oats, is my favorite grass, and I put it in a prominent position next to a variegated iris. The flat seedheads are exquisite and should be placed so that they can be seen easily.

Deschampsia caespitosa, tufted hair grass, is unusual in that it will take some shade. Needs good drainage.

Festuca glauca, blue fescue. There are many named varieties in this family, some smaller than others. Makes a little blue tuft that looks like a cloud.

Hakonechloa macra 'Aureola' is a brilliant yellow grass that looks as if the wind is perpetually riffling through it. Splendid in a pot, superb as an edger. It tolerates some shade, but if you have trouble with this one, move it into more sun. I find that it puts up with fairly adverse conditions.

Helictotrichon sempervirens, blue oat grass, is a steely blue and looks gorgeous all winter long. In spring, cut it back to about 2 inches from the ground, and it will start growing back very quickly. It divides easily in spring as well.

Luzula nivea, snowy wood rush. A low-growing, pale-edged plant that will take some shade and has an almost grasslike effect. Drought-tolerant.

Ophiopogon planiscapus 'Nigrescens,' black mondo grass, really is black and in a pale container shows itself for the beauty it is. No matter where you put this strange plant, make sure it has a pale background, or it will simply disappear.

Panicum virgatum, switch grass, forms clumps and grows to about 3 feet in my garden; the panicles turn from bronze to purple as the weather gets cold. It stays a strong yellow all winter.

FERNS

Ferns can be used in containers, but they look best in

combination with hostas and groundcovers, such as pulmonarias and lamiums. I adore ferns of all sorts, and a few pots of them will make any dank, miserable corner into a thing of beauty.

Adiantum pedatum, maidenhair fern, is an exquisite, moisture- and acid-loving plant.

Asplenium platyneuron, ebony spleenwort, is evergreen and good for any spot with a little light. *A. trichomanes*, maidenhair spleenwort, makes a good background plant.

Polystichum acrostichoides, Christmas fern, needs dappled shade and will grow to 3 feet.

Woodsia alpina is evergreen and really small at 4 inches; fronds have irregular margins.

SEDUMS AND SEMPERVIVUMS

Sedums
Sedums can be propagated by snipping off a stem, pushing it into prepared ground and watering. They like sunny, dry conditions; otherwise, they flop about. There are dozens of species of groundcovering sedums, but I like these clump formers in the autumn garden.

S. maximum 'Atropurpureum' is a deep, interesting purple with pink flowers. It can reach almost 2 feet.

S. spathulifolium 'Purpureum,' a great favorite, is a lovely spreader and doesn't get too tall.

S. 'Vera Jameson' has deep purple and blue foliage that works as well in a container as in the ground. Has dark pink blooms.

S. 'Autumn Joy' is the most widely used for good reason: It forms a handsome clump that has pink flowers in autumn.

S. spectabile 'Variegatum' has variegated fleshy stems and pink flowers in autumn.

Sempervivums

You've got to have semps somewhere in the garden, especially in shallow containers. Fondly known as hens-and-chicks, they will crawl all over the surface of a stone or concrete container or trough. If you keep them through the winter, put them in a spot protected from both wind and moisture. Mine survive under the shelter of a table on the deck. To propagate, pull off one of the little offsets and stick it in soil. It will become the mother plant. Just make sure that semps have good drainage. Place them so that it's possible to see the subtle leaf forms and edgings. You can create an entire semp garden by using a slope facing south, filling it with sand and some topsoil, then putting in everything you can find. This is a plant that's absolutely wonderful for trading and for using on a balcony (won't get windblasted) and in containers to make a miniature landscape. Combine with fleshy-leaved annuals such as echeverias.

PERENNIALS

Any garden, including the pocket garden, is going to comprise mainly perennials. Most need little care and thrive if they are mulched in spring and autumn to keep them safe from severe changes in temperature. This also holds back weeds. Weeds are the scourge of the small garden, they are so obvious. I like crawling around in the spring and getting out as many as I possibly can while the soil is still very moist. This list of perennials is short, but they are all plants I particularly like because they are hardy and they don't succumb to bugs or disease easily. You can try anything as long as it isn't invasive, doesn't get overwhelmingly large and is easy to cultivate.

Arabis caucasica, rock cress, a foaming white groundcover in spring, with gray-green serrated leaves the rest of the time. To get rid of the seedheads, just snap them out with a quick twist of the wrist.

Armeria maritima, thrift, needs well-drained soil; great for a scree garden with its attractive, little hummock covered with flowers. Plant high.

Artemisia pontica or *A. ludoviciana* 'Silver King' or 'Valerie Finnis,' all of which might be invasive in other parts of the garden, do okay here in the most adverse conditions. *A. camphorata* is superb but requires lots of pruning. *A. absinthium* 'Huntington' is currently my favorite, and I've found it to be slightly hardier than the popular *A.* 'Powis Castle,' but they share the silver, lacy foliage that is invaluable in any garden. *A. schmidtiana* 'Silver Mound' is feathery and more rounded. *A. dracunculus*, tarragon, is a bit floppy, so I prefer to keep it in pots. For a shrubbier form, try *A. lactiflora* 'Guizho.' It has white flowers and is utterly hardy.

16

Keith Squires' scree garden is an example of xeroscape gardening at its best. See page 153 for a complete plant list.

17

Amy and Clair Stewart's garden has many parts. This brilliantly constructed stone wall is home to campanulas, sedums and sempervivums. See page 158.

18 Larry Davidson's garden at his nursery, Lost Horizons, has pockets throughout that serve as excellent models. Some of the plants he uses: *Epimedium rubra, Festuca glauca* and sedums. See page 155.

Asarum europaeum, European ginger, is a handsome groundcover with shiny, dark green leaves. Slow to start and then it takes off. Divides easily. Looks great under shrubs.

Aster spp. *A. x frikartii* is early, blue and perfect; 'Wonder of Staefa' and 'Moench' are the two most readily available. *A. alpinus* is another good species for the pocket garden. *A. tongolensis* reaches about 18 inches in the sun.

Bergenia cordifolia is an evergreen groundcover with large leaves that won't grow out of bounds. Good edger that turns a wonderful magenta in winter.

Campanula spp. There's no such thing as a bad campanula, and most of them will fit just perfectly in a pocket of space. *C. carpatica* 'Blue Clips' and 'White Clips' are great mounds of bloom that return with deadheading (true of most campanulas). Other species to look at: *C. lactiflora, C. persicifolia, C. portenschlagiana* and *C. rotundifolia.*

Ceratostigma plumbaginoides. It's a slow groundcover that turns vermilion in autumn over brilliant blue flowers.

Coreopsis verticillata 'Moonbeam.' Pale yellow is always a welcome addition. No problems with this one.

Corydalis flexuosa 'Blue Panda' will bring any visitor to a dead halt. *C. f.* 'China Blue' is even more intense.

Dicentra eximia 'Luxuriant,' bleeding heart, blooms and blooms and blooms with magenta or rose flowers over dissected gray-green leaves.

Gentiana septemfida. Magnificent, cobalt-blue bloom in August. Will take some shade.

Geranium spp., cranesbills, are hard to deal with in a small garden. 'Johnson's Blue' is constantly misidentified, and you can end up with a field of huge blue *G. pratense*—just don't get involved. *G. grandiflorum* (this is also sold as *G. himalayense*) is an intense, deep blue and grows to about 18 inches. There are dozens of other hardy geraniums for the small garden, but not *G. macrorrhizum*, which will spread too quickly. *G. renardii* has a rugose foliage I like; *G. cinereum* 'Ballerina' is a pretty little clump former with long-blooming pink flowers with darker pink striations.

Gillenia trifoliata is a great plant that will grow in sun or shade, good or bad soil. White, starlike flowers with an orange foliage change in autumn.

Heuchera, coral bells, are now among the most versatile plants you can have in a small garden. Because of the advances in tissue culture, there are whole new generations of colors and performance that come out every year. If you look at 'Palace Purple' and think that's the only magenta leaf heuchera, you're missing 'Chocolate Ruffles,' 'Pewter Veil' and 'Stormy Seas,' and a range of greens and silvers that's mind-boggling. Plant them slightly above the ground, don't mulch close to the center of the plant, and cut out anything that looks ratty almost any time of the year. As an edger, it can't be beat.

Hosta spp. It's great to have hostas in the small garden but read the labels. Anything that gets bigger than 1 foot is going to be a giant in really good conditions. If they have too much shade, they'll be a haven for slugs. I like the following: *H.* 'Blue Cadet,' 'Halcyon,' or 'Blue Lake.' The bright yellow edger hostas, 'Limelight,' 'Gold Edger,' 'Feather Boa' and 'Golden Sceptre,' are invaluable. Then there's the variegation of 'Ginko Craig.' Be careful with this plant. If you are in doubt, use it in a container—a big one.

Iris pallida 'Variegata' is not only choice in appearance, you can't kill it. It doesn't get all messy, divides easily and has the kind of foliage that goes with anything. Even produces a pale blue, scented flower—for about 10 minutes. Appreciate it while you can.

Kirengeshoma palmata and *K. koreana* are both subtle, with exquisite yellow trumpets (albeit very small ones) hanging from attractive, maplelike leaves.

Lamium, deadnettle, another family of plants that are being developed so quickly that it's hard to keep up with the cultivars. *L. maculatum* 'White Nancy' is a lovely pale leaf with white flowers. They need little or no work except to divide and share once they've done the job of being a good groundcovering.

Lavandula angustifolia, lavender, 'Hidcote' and 'Munstead' are the two hardiest in my experience. They will live in pots, in the ground, and may get chopped down by winter. But simply prune them to where you see some growth in spring, and they will bounce back. Or they can be left alone for many years. Harvest the flowers just as they break open. Put them among your best woolens, and they'll repel moths.

Pulmonaria saccharata, lungwort. There are so many you can almost become a collector. Blooms range from blue to pink, often on the same stem. Named forms include 'Peaches and Cream,' 'David Ward' and 'Mrs. Moon,' which has pink flowers. *P. longifolia* 'Roy Davidson' and 'Bertram Anderson' have long, graceful leaves mottled with silver or pewter, and blue flowers.

Rosa 'The Fairy' may sound like a horrendous cliché, but for value for space, this little pink bush rose is the best. For other small shrub roses, try *R. bonica*, a gorgeous little rose, or *R. polyantha* 'White Pet,' which is disease-resistant and has a good habit. For saving space, look for climbers. Cut out any dead canes in spring; keep them attached to fences very loosely so that they won't flop about. *R.* 'Reine Victoria,' a tall, floppy Bourbon rose, looks perfect when it's tied up. My rose maven bends the laterals to one side and ties them onto the supports, and they bloom all along the canes. *R. centifolia* 'Fantin-Latour' is another good one. 'Coral Dawn' never gets too large (it's smaller than the beautiful but vigorous 'New Dawn').

Rosmarinus, rosemary, is either an indoor plant to be taken out in summer or a perennial if you live in a warm area. There are at least a dozen new named forms that are worth trying. No garden should be without a pot of this highly scented plant. If it gets hit with a little frost in the autumn, it won't kill a container plant.

Sagina subulata, Irish moss. It isn't really a moss but looks like one and will grow anywhere you want. Has tiny white flowers.

Salvia officinalis, sage, the only herb I couldn't do without. It looks marvelous, and I love it in cooking. But there are plenty of salvias in many different species that are right for the pocket garden. *S. verticillata* 'Purple Rain' is a splendid, deep red-purple.

Sidalcea candida, white checker mallow or little hollyhock, is a great, 3-foot plant that will bloom for months if deadheaded. It makes a perfect drift, and I haven't found it to get out of bounds.

Thymus, thyme, has so many good cultivars that it's another collector's item. *T. montanus* are ground-huggers with white or pink flowers; *T. x citriodorus* is lemon-scented, gold-edged. *T.* 'E.B. Anderson' has a golden color all winter; *T. pseudolanuginosus,* woolly thyme, has soft gray fuzzy foliage that looks wonderful next to rocks. The montanas will make small clumps and come in pinks and white.

Yucca filamentosa, Adam's needle, is a very striking plant, and there are some extraordinary cultivars. I like 'Bright Edge,' which has strong green spikes with a soft silver edging.

INVASIVES

These are the plants that should be used only in

containers; otherwise, you'll have them all over your garden and spend most of your time hauling them out again. Nevertheless, they are useful plants and should not be ignored.

Aegopodium podagraria 'Variegatum,' variegated goutweed, is about the most invasive plant I know. It looks pretty, with small leaves of pale green outlined in white, but left to its own devices, it will choke out everything else in the garden. Ah, but put it in a big pot and plunge it into a shady corner, and you've got a good plant. Please don't use it in any other way.

Cerastium tomentosum, snow-in-summer, looks good in and out of bloom in a window box. Gray foliage, luminous white flowers.

Cryptotaenia japonica is a wonderfully hardy plant (Zone 4) that looks great with its purplish black foliage in deep shade. It has white flowers and will self-seed everywhere. Magnificent in pots.

Elymus glaucus, blue lyme grass. I would never put this anywhere but in a big container, preferably a huge tin pot plunged into the ground. This is a great-looking plant but unbelievably invasive.

Lysimachia nummularia, creeping Jenny. Bright yellow flowers in even the darkest shade. This one can get out of hand after a few years, but it will do its job to protect exposed soil. Keep it in a container. Try *L. n.* 'Aurea' or *L. congestifolia* 'Outback Sunset' with lemon yellow flowers and golden-green foliage. The golden form is, blessedly, a shade lover that doesn't grow nearly as rapidly as the green, and I use it to edge borders as well as in pots.

Mentha suaveolens, pineapple mint, is light green with cream edging.

BULBS

I'm partial to all small bulbs no matter what color. If you plant hundreds and hundreds, even in confined spaces, eventually you'll get a good show.

Chionodoxa luciliae, glory-of-the-snow, is low-growing, has blue flowers with starry, white centers and naturalizes beautifully.

Fritillaria meleagris, a late bloomer, has drooping purple bells. I also like a weirder-looking one called *F. michailovskyi,* which has an amazing little face of purple and yellow.

Muscari armeniacum, grape hyacinth. It's impossible to have too many of these brilliant blue spikes on 8-inch stems. 'Blue Spike' has double blue at the top.

Narcissus such as 'Pipit,' 'February Gold' and the glorious white 'Thalia' all fit into small spaces.

Scilla siberica and *S. hyacinthoides* are both stunning in containers, rock gardens and borders with their deep blues. You need plenty.

Tulipa kaufmanniana. Small and exquisite, they are good for both containers and anywhere else in the pocket garden. *T. tarda* is a favorite species, with upward-facing pale cream petals centered with yellow; *T. turkestanica,* another species, has gray-green leaves and clusters of flowers with a white interior and yellow heart. *T. batalinii,* single, soft yellow. A late bloomer which is stunning is *T.* 'Spring Green.'

ANNUALS

Many of the wonderful annuals listed below are excellent plants for containers and hanging baskets. Trailers are good for either hanging baskets or for ground-covers in containers. Annuals will carry on until frost in most cases. They require deadheading so that they won't go to seed, regular watering and a light feeding of diluted fish emulsion fertilizer every few weeks during the summer.

Agapanthus, lily-of-the-Nile, 3 feet, white or blue bloom. Survives in a pot for years if you fertilize lightly during the flowering period. 'Lilliput' is a dwarf form.

Antirrhinum 'Clownerie White,' creeping snapdragon, has silver foliage and white flowers. This is a gorgeous pot plant.

Argyranthemum frutescens 'White Lace' is a form of marguerite daisy which I adore. The daisylike white flowers and ferny, blue-green foliage are choice.

Bacopa 'Snowflake' or 'Pink Domino.' This plant is ideal for any container. It trails, has dark green foliage and gets smothered with white or pink flowers if it's watered regularly.

Bidens ferulifolia. Yellow flowers, charming, threadleaf foliage, and it blooms on and on during the season.

Brachycome 'Ultra,' Swan River daisy, in a bright blue with ferny foliage.

Calocephalus brownii, cushion bush. Leafless stems of bright silver form dense mounds. Background plant for others with bright flowers. From Australia.

Clivia, kaffir lily. Likes to be pot-bound. Fertilize in spring and summer, dry out in autumn to set flower production in motion; orange flowers with yellow centers.

Coleus. There is now a whole new breed of these old-fashioned foliage plants. They can go in containers or in a shady corner and brighten up just about any place you can think of. 'The Line' has chartreuse to golden-green leaves with a dark burgundy stripe down the middle; 'Chantilly Lace' has red, ruffled leaves with green edge; 'Victorian Ruffles' sports bright green stems and purple leaves splashed pink. 'Black Dragon' and 'Purple Emperor' are deep burgundy.

Convolvulus 'Morning Trails.' A miniature form with pale blue, morning-glorylike blooms that go on all summer.

Cosmos 'White Sensation.' Who can resist such a lovely, self-seeding annual? And this one at 18 inches is particularly good with shining white petals. Try the tender form, *C. atrosanguineus,* chocolate cosmos—unbelievable.

Eucharis, Amazon lily, can flower throughout the year. Dark green strappy leaves, white flowers (sort of like a daffodil), scented; can be pot-bound for a number of years; don't place in direct sun; likes lots of indirect light, warmth and humidity.

Evolvulus 'Blue Haze' has silvery-green foliage with smashing blue flowers.

Fuchsia 'Thalia,' has no protruding stamens and looks more refined than the blowsier forms. 'Lottie Hobbie' has tiny, vivid pink flowers and is much smaller than the normal ones. Check these plants out if you haven't before.

Helichrysum petiolare is the most useful of all plants in this category. It has soft, silvery leaves and will romp and bound about if it's planted directly in soil. In a pot, it will climb or drip, depending on what you want or need. *H. p.* 'Limelight' and 'Variegatum' are acid-yellow, the latter with softer gray margins. This is another plant that's variously identified as 'variegated,' green edged with gold; another variegated 'Limelight' came as yellow-edged with gray. This is a murky area. Just try to get the best variegations you can.

Heliotropium peruvianum, cherry-pie. A shrubby plant with either intense purple or white flowers with a light scent; excellent for containers or as a bedding plant.

Ipomoea batatas 'Blackie' has dark purple, almost black foliage. It's gorgeous.

Lobelia 'Crystal Palace.' Its cobalt-blue flowers will shine even in the shade.

Lotus berthelotii. Gray, feathery foliage with yellow and orange beak-shaped flowers.

Mimulus aurantiacus. Shrubby with soft orange flowers and shiny foliage.

Nemesia 'Innocence' (white); 'Confetti' (light mauve-pink); 'Joan Wilder' (deep pink). These plants have a snapdragonlike bloom, and some forms are fragrant.

Nemophila menziesii, baby blue eyes. Wonderful blue flowers with white centers.

Nicotiana sylvestris and *N. alata.* Don't get the hybrids; stick to one of the highly scented ones that release their fragrance in the evening.

Pelargonium 'Crocodile' is an ivy geranium that is an almost chlorotic lime-green, deeply veined with maroon.

Plectranthus argentatus. This is a great container plant with gray foliage, purple stems and light mauve flowers. Any form of plectranthus is going to give good value. Why not try a different one: *P. zuliensis,* which starts off looking kind of boring but, by summer, has purple stems, green foliage and spikes of blue-mauve flowers; *P. fosteri* 'Ochre Flame'; or other forms in variegated limes, greens, gray or golden colors.

Plumbago capensis has a long, trailing habit with phloxlike flowers. I love it almost anywhere, partly because of the quality of the blue.

Sanvitalia procumbens, creeping zinnia, is a clinger for the shade with burgundy stems, golden flowers and dark green leaves.

Scaevola 'Blue Wonder.' What a great plant. It has bright blue flowers over stiff, dark green foliage, and it goes on for months and months just looking better. Use everywhere in the garden.

Tibouchina urvilleana, glory bush. Shrubby with silvery foliage and deep, purple-blue flowers.

Tropaeolum, nasturtium, especially 'Helen Long,' with double apricot flowers, is a stunner; there are also climbing and variegated versions of this useful annual, which prefers poor soil.

Verbena 'Homestead Purple' is a trailer for the sun; ferny foliage; resistant to mildew.

Viola hederacea. This trailing viola forms flat mats of green foliage topped by blue and white flowers. Could be a groundcover as well.

Wedelia trilobata, golden creeping daisy, is a quick-growing trailer for the shade with dark green leaves and yellow to orange daisylike flowers.

Bibliography

Baxendale, Martin. *Gardening in Miniature*. New York: Sterling, 1990.

Berry, Susan, and Steve Bradley. *Contained Gardens: Creative Designs and Projects*. Pownall, VT: Storey Publishing, 1995.

Binetti, Marianne. *Shortcuts for Accenting Your Garden*. Pownall, VT: Storey Publishing, 1993.

——*Tips for Carefree Landscapes*. Pownall, VT: Storey Publishing, 1990.

Bird, Richard, and John Kelly. *The Complete Book of Alpine Gardening*. London: Villiers House, 1992.

Boisset, Caroline. *Vertical Gardening*. New York: Grove Weidenfeld, 1988.

Charlesworth, Geoffrey. *The Opinionated Gardener: Random Offshoots from an Alpine Garden*. Boston: David R. Godine, 1988.

——*A Gardener Obsessed: Observations, Reflections, and Advice for Other Dedicated Gardeners*. Boston: David R. Godine, 1994.

Fisher, Sue. *The Hanging Garden: Creative Display for Every Garden*. London: Headline Books, 1995.

Harrad, Julie. *The Garden Wall, Fences, and Hedges: Their Planning and Planting.* New York: The Atlantic Monthly Press, 1991.

Ingerwersen, Will. *Alpines in Colour.* London: Villiers House, 1991.

Ortho Books. *Gardening in Containers.* San Raman, CA: Ortho Books, 1984.

Rae-Smith, William. *The Complete Book of Water Gardening.* London: Bestseller Publishing, 1989.

Rose, Graham. *The Small Garden Planner.* New York: Simon and Schuster, 1987.

Sears, Elayne (illus.). *Step-by-Step Gardening Techniques Illustrated.* Pownall, VT: Storey Publishing, 1995.

Tarling, Thomasina. *Truly Tiny Gardens.* London: Conran/Octopus Books, 1995.

Van Sweden, James and Wolfgang Oehme. *Gardening with Water.* Toronto: Random House of Canada, 1995.

Yang, Linda. *The City Gardener's Handbook: From Balcony to Backyard.* New York: J.M. Dent & Sons, 1990.

Index